Cat Chat

Bébé was sitting on the windowsill watching, waiting. I hurried to the boutique, borrowed a chair and climbed up to try to kiss him. The window was half closed, so I banged my nose hard, but it didn't matter. Unable to kiss Bébé, I slid my hand inside to the ledge where he was sitting, caressed his neck and told him how I'd missed him and how he was still the most beautiful cat in the world. Then, before returning to the house to unpack, I promised to pass by late on when he would be sitting on the roof taking the fresh night air . . . When I entered Bébé's street, I saw him sitting on the roof, outlined against a navy night sky. I called out, 'Good-night, Bébé, see you in the morning.' And he miaowed, as if in reply, as he always had. Then he ran along the flat roof so he could miaow again when I turned to wave before disappearing from view.

Hélène Thornton is a writer and artist. She was born in Blackpool and lived in nine countries before settling in La Cadière d'Azur in the Var region of Provence. The first time she owned a cat was at the age of 21, when she rescued a kitten that had been hit by a car. Her husband says she is part cat.

CAT CHAT

Hélène Thornton

This paperback edition first published in 2001 by
Virgin Publishing Ltd
Thames Wharf Studios
Rainville Road
London
W6 9HA

First published in Great Britain in 2000 by Virgin Publishing Ltd

A catalogue record for this book is available from the British Library.

ISBN 0 7535 0522 3

Phototypeset by Intype London Ltd
Printed and bound in Great Britain by Mackays of Chatham plc

For 'Monsieur'

PART ONE

PART ONE

The Cat Matchmaker

'God made the cat so man could have a tiger
to stroke at home.'
Victor Hugo

Prologue

Southern France, autumn

The cat was small, part gutter variety, part Abyssinian,
with big ears like a desert fox, and a comic expression.
Sitting in the sun, her back against the grey stone walls
of an old village house, she was almost invisible. She
seemed to be dozing, but from time to time she opened
her big green eyes and had a quick look around.

Pausing to stroke her, I earned a contented purr. Then
I entered the antique shop next to her wall, impressed
by château-sized furniture, church relics and iron fire
backs from long ruined mansions that no one but a
millionaire could afford. I could just find the money for
a giant pair of Victorian knickers, to be used as shorts
someday. Emerging into the crisp autumn air, I saw a
tourist release his dog and urge it towards the little cat.
Unable to speak French, I shouted an involuntary 'No!
No!' The cat woke, rose up and arched her back in the
feline battle position.

A small crowd formed as the dog closed in. I had never felt as helpless as I did that day, watching the dog advance for the kill. Then everything happened with lightning speed. The dog neared Big Ears, till he was as close as a whisper. One minute the cat was still and silent. Then she let out a blood-curdling series of howls worthy of a troupe of Gurkhas in full charge and sprang at the dog, her claws raking his face, once, twice, till he ran away, howling with pain.

Calm as a judge, the cat returned to her place against the wall and I went and sat on the rock next to her, my heart thundering from anger and fear and relief. The tourist walked towards me, visibly furious and cried out, 'Your cat attacked my dog!'

The watchers shouted him down and he hurried away, his face the picture of disappointment. As the crowd dispersed, I looked the cat over to make sure she was unharmed. I kept thinking about the dog, who had been encouraged to attack her and who had ended up badly injured. Despite the cat's impressive defence of her life, I felt very down. The incident had upset my idea of how we live in a so-called civilised society. Had the man hated the cat just because she was a cat? Or did he just love to hate? Or was he one who dreamed of destroying, like the Daleks in *Doctor Who*? He hadn't had the courage to kill the cat himself, so he'd sent his dog to do it.

The church clock struck four. Having given the cat a last kiss or two or three, I turned towards the tiny apartment I'd just rented and came face to face with a tall, white-haired man of military bearing, who had been there when I entered the antique shop. He didn't speak, just looked with great intensity into my face before moving on.

When I entered the village house, whose attic floor would be mine for the next few weeks, Madame Bere, my landlady, exclaimed '*Mon Dieu, regarde comme Madame est pale.*' Looking in the mirror, I saw that I was indeed a whiter shade of pale. Madame Bere called for her husband to bring the vin d'orange. I'd never heard of orange wine and assumed it was some kind of fruit cordial. After six hours of driving, then lifting my luggage and an eighteen-kilo IBM antiquity up three flights of stairs, I was indeed thirsty. So I drank it down, surprised to be scolded by Madame.

'Hélène, you must *sip* vin d'orange! It's very strong, you know.'

I sipped the second glass, thanked them both and then walked slowly upstairs. I'm not used to drinking wine and I was surprised to feel an overwhelming desire for an hour in bed. Having flopped down, I lay back fully clothed, without unpacking my cases, and woke the following morning at eight, appalled to have slept with clothes and make-up on for the first time in my life. From that moment on, vin d'orange was put on my list of forbidden pleasures along with pastis, greasy sausages and cream!

That was my first afternoon in the south and the seeds of destiny had been sown by a little cat and an oaf with a big dog. I didn't realise it at the time, but, in the pale sunlight of autumn, my future had been written on an ancient, grey stone wall.

Chapter One

The village was very old and full of tourists in summer. In autumn and winter visitors came mainly at week-ends. My apartment was unusual, under the eaves and comprising a tiny bathroom and large loftlike kitchen cum living room cum bedroom. I was alone, apart from a lizard with lace-like feet, immediately christened Lenny Lizard. Lenny formed the habit of appearing each morning when I cleaned my teeth and often gave me a demonstration about teatime of his talent for catching flies.

For the first three days, I slept, exhausted by the long journey to this fairy-tale village in the Midi. Then I began to establish my routines. These went haywire on the fifth day after my arrival, when, having made the early-morning tea, I pulled back the curtains to let in the light – and froze. Outside, everything was white. The mimosas were heavy, laden with snow, the eucalyptus likewise. Nothing stirred under an icy pink sky. It had snowed in the Midi.

At first I was furious and thought of leaving immediately. Then I realised that I couldn't, because the road down would be impossible to negotiate in heavy snow conditions. I closed the curtains, put more logs on the fire and began to work. Work is my antidote for all things horrible, even snow in the Midi.

The snow and its aftereffects lasted less than a week. Everything came to a halt because there were no snowploughs available to clear motorways, and many travellers and long-distance lorry drivers were forced to seek shelter in private homes, hotels, motels and hastily improvised church halls. I learned a lesson that I should have learned years previously: that in Europe winter sun is hard to find. Still, I was working and feeling well and I decided to pay my next visit to the area in the middle of summer. Then, at least, I could be certain that the landscape would seem to oscillate in the ferocious heat and everything would be golden.

When the snow disappeared a few days later, I began to explore the village. My first port of call was the local café, its terrace sheltered by the branches of a Chinese mulberry tree. I formed the habit of visiting the café for coffee each morning and had my special table, near the fire, where I corrected the previous night's writing. One morning, short-sighted as always, I bumped into the tall white-haired man as I passed the counter en route to my table. I didn't notice him in the sombre lit entrance, but said, *'Excusez moi, monsieur,'* to be polite. He never forgot the moment of impact. I didn't remember it till some years later.

Outside the boutique of Madame Bere's daughter, I met a grey tomcat with fur like velvet, Gastounet, who bit me the moment I stopped stroking him. Mediterranean cats, like men of the region, are spoiled to death by the women in their lives. The men prefer dogs, the bigger the better to make them look like Rambo. But French women like cats and some of them *look* like cats with their wonderful eyes and feline way of moving. Madame Bere said I must give Gastounet a little piece of ham or chicken to compensate for the fact that I'd stopped stroking him. 'That way, he won't think of biting you in case he doesn't get his ham.'

The village houses were of grey stone, their walls clothed by flowering creepers: plumbago with its pale-blue flowers, jasmine and the fiery beauty of Virginia Creeper. And sometimes, as I walked, I felt eyes watching me and, looking up, saw a line of fat tabby cats assessing and deciding whether I was worth cultivating. They had, no doubt, learned these ways from their masters, who often stayed for hours outside the bars, watching the world go by and accepting or not accepting newcomers. In the Midi it takes a long time to merit acceptance.

I was emerging from a flower-clad arch, when I saw a sign BROCANTE. This is the French equivalent of a minor-level antique dealer, selling mainly bric-a-brac and different periods of small furniture not usually of interest to a reputed dealer. Entering the open room I said 'Good morning' to the owner, who was sitting in a very comfortable-looking armchair. Then I inspected the pieces, asking the price from time to time, but the man didn't reply. At that moment I saw a beautiful tapestry cushion covered in beads and asked joyfully what the price was. The owner didn't reply, just got up and stirred a pan that was bubbling, incongruously, on a gas ring at the far end of the room. Exasperated by his look of disbelief and refusal to reply, I spoke sharply.

'Do you want to sell or not?'

He replied in a very tiny voice, 'This is my home madame, it's not a shop.'

And we laughed together at my error and he telephoned his brother, who telephoned half the village to tell them that an English lady had entered Raymond and Fanny's living room and had tried to buy a vase and a bead-covered cushion! Suddenly people wanted to say good morning. They couldn't say my name, Thornton, because the French can't put their tongue in the right place to say the 'th'. So I told everyone to call me Hélène, which they could say. I did not realise that in France this simply isn't done. But pragmatism won and they called me Hélène to avoid long and frustrating lessons in saying 'th'.

As time passed, my habit of walking for half an hour each morning and the same at the end of each afternoon was noticed and commented on by the residents. Sometimes, the little cat who lived next to the antique shop came to walk with me. Then Gastounet took to following, enjoying most of all a brief stop at the end of the walk for him to devour a slice of ham in the pizzeria. I didn't know that the French detest walking and so my habits seemed very odd indeed, particularly as the village streets were steep and cobbled. The fact that I was often followed by three or four cats that didn't belong to me was probably taken for English eccentricity.

My walks always ended when I passed an ancient street where my favourite house was situated. It was a house like all the others, but this one had a plus: a black and white cat of astonishing beauty, who sat in the window, looking out. He was the most beautiful cat I had ever seen and I often approached on tiptoe and made a little sign to him as he sat like Machiavelli's

Prince behind the window. '*Tu es le plus beau chat du monde*,' I said, making an effort to speak French, because he was a French cat. He made no sign of having heard and I stayed there, just gazing at him, hypnotised by his presence and his beauty.

One day, Monsieur Bere passed by as I was talking to the beautiful animal and commented that the cat never went out of the house, because his owner feared his being attacked by the dogs belonging to tourists. That I could well understand, but I didn't think imprisonment was the answer either. 'Don't you worry about him,' Marcel Bere reassured me. 'He goes on the flat roof of the house and into the winter garden and then he patrols all the flat rooftops of the other houses nearby. If Bébé went into the Olympics he'd win a gold medal for the high jump, the long jump and having his own way.'

With that Marcel continued on towards the grocery store, leaving me more bewitched than ever by the cat. As always, I went to the window, stood on tiptoe and whispered, '*Tu es le plus beau chat du monde, et je t'aime.*' That day, I was unaware that the owner of the cat was standing directly behind me listening as he waited to mount the steps to his home.

One night, when I couldn't sleep, I dressed and went for a solitary stroll in the village centre. Arriving in the square in front of the Town Hall, in former times a stone castle, I saw a strange sight: at least a dozen village cats sitting here and there in the moonlit clearing, intoning strange, moaning, chanting sounds. It was a cross between a Greek chorus and a meeting of a village council of elders. None moved. There was no sign of hostility, harmony or any human emotion, just a feline communication of obvious importance and mounting crescendo. As I sat in a dark corner watching them, I realised that cats communicate by tone, volume, harmony and some mysterious almost musical timing.

I was about to leave when I felt the little cat with big ears sitting next to me. She was silent, watchful, part of the meeting and yet distant from it. When I whispered to her, she purred and we stayed there long after the others had dispersed. Finally, I walked back to my apartment via the street and the house of the beautiful cat and there, outlined against the night sky, I saw him on the roof. It was too late to call to him, so I whispered an English goodnight and heard an answering, plaintive miaow. It was our first communication and a precious one.

I had passed the house every day and always found the cat there, alone, watching the world pass by and dreaming of joining it. When tourists shouted, 'What a lovely cat!', as if the world and its brother were stone deaf, Bébé jumped down from the windowsill, returning only when the savages had gone. Marcel Bere had told me that Bébé's owner was out most days from mid-morning to early evening. He had a boat and loved sea fishing. Bébé was therefore very lonely. I was lonely too and this made me feel a close bond with the most beautiful cat in the world.

Friday morning was market day. I loved the big, unruly bunches of flowers, the masses of tiger lilies that smelled of my nana's house, a precious memory from childhood. I bought fruit, vegetables, eggs and lilies, stopped for a coffee in the market stall café and then returned, baskets full, to the village. As in most tourist villages in France, residents are obliged to keep their cars outside between eight in the morning and seven at night, tough going when you're carrying heavy things.

Walking slowly through the ancient portico and up the steep street towards the apartment, I felt a cricket jump down the bodice of my dress. Terrified, I loosened the belt and shook everything I had to make it go away, provoking a group of village men into howls of laughter. Then, when I was sure it had gone, I continued up the hill, coming face to face with a very large beige car, its driver invisible due to the reflections of the wintery sun on the windscreen. As his fat car filled the width of the street, I had to climb up the steps of a nearby house to avoid getting flattened. Scowling at the invisible driver, who moved on at a stately pace, I continued on my way, saying to a passing friend that people who drive huge, old-fashioned cars in the narrow village streets are pompous old farts.

Time passed too fast in the ancient village. My work was finished and I knew it was time to return home to Ireland. I'd been trying very hard to learn French during my stay, by the unconventional method of reading *Tristesse et Beauté* by Kawabata, translated from the Japanese into French. Every night I'd written down the words I'd had to look up in the dictionary and had learned them like Polly Parrot. The result was a spectacular vocabulary in French but a total incapacity to conjugate even the simplest verb. Still, I'd made friends and, as I packed my bags for the return, I felt unaccountably sad. I'd been travelling for a quarter of a century, arriving and leaving without regret. So why, I wondered, did I feel so troubled by the thought of leaving this village behind?

I walked past the antique shop and gave a last kiss to Big Ears, the cat. I went for a coffee to the café and kissed everyone goodbye. Then, finally, I walked towards my favourite house to see the beautiful cat.

He was sitting in the window, magnificent as ever, but looking a bit dejected. The window was slightly open, though secured on a metal hook. Having borrowed a chair from the boutique nearby, I climbed up so I could stroke his ears. This lasted a long time and he made little noises when I talked to him. I left with the greatest regret, looking back until I could no longer see him, only hear his sad miaow.

Poor Bébé. He was obviously well housed and nourished but, oh, so alone. I wondered why his master couldn't take him out in the car or on his boat. Did he not realise that cats like company? I'd told Bébé that I would come back in the summertime to see him, but that left months of solitude, when he would pine in silence for a friend. I decided to get the local schoolmaster, who spoke English, to write to me telling me how Bébé was getting on. That would stop me worrying myself to death about his condition and would ensure that if necessary I could get Martine, the owner of the café, to go and see Monsieur to warn him if the cat lost weight or appeared to be depressed. I was already thinking of Bébé as my personal responsibility and had to correct this tendency by reminding myself that he belonged to someone else.

Three days later, I arrived in Dublin and made my way to the southwest, where they were suffering a heat wave. All my friends were convinced that the dehydration caused by profuse sweating could be fatal, so they drank twice as much as usual. Bars filled with Guinness, lager and poteen swiggers and there was no shortage of bars because the Irish are true originals. Where else do you find a bar in the back room of the grocer's, the draper's, the newspaper shop and the funeral parlour (though I never checked that one out!)?

For the moment, I was content to be home and delighted to put on a swimsuit. That first afternoon, I got out the sunchair and lay back to bronze in County Galway. After snow in the Midi, it was delicious.

Chapter Two

Monsieur Duval, the schoolmaster, was fifty years old, a small round gentleman with a passion for cats, bonsai and women with red hair. He was very proud of his English, learned first as a youth when he had gone hitchhiking for three months to the States. At the end of three months he had found work in a Chinese laundry in San Francisco and had stayed another few months as an illegal immigrant, the only time he had broken the law in his entire life. The stay in America had perfected his English, if with a slightly singsong accent that was the result of his experiences in the Chinese laundry. At that time, the adventure was almost unique for a Frenchman and Monsieur Duval was considered a very cosmopolitan type, even though he had rarely left the village since. His letters were very serious and often unintentionally funny.

Madame Hélène,

I am sorry to have to tell you that this week Bébé had to be taken to the vet. He has lost weight and refuses to eat and on Wednesday last he bit Monsieur. The vet said there was nothing seriously wrong with the cat but that Bébé is bored and needs to play and have surprises. Monsieur was very upset, partly because he doesn't know how to surprise a cat and, as he is out most of the day, he doesn't find time to play with Bébé.

Are you returning soon? I am sure when he sees you again Bébé will regain his appetite and you will give him a surprise every single day, like you did my wife and I when you walked up the hill to the château in your gold shoes with ten centimetre heels. We still laugh about that.

I have nothing else to tell you. My rheumatism is very painful at the moment, but summer is almost here, so I am confident that soon I will feel better. Do write and tell us when you will return and if there is anything we can do for you. My wife and her sister send their regards as I do.

With respect.

Henri Duval.

P.S. I have just been informed that the apartment in the home of Madame Bere is free because of the early departure of the previous tenant. Do you wish me to reserve it for you? Please tell me immediately.

I packed my things, including my current novel files and everything I consider indispensable to daily life – such as books, bedsocks, perfume and Rochas cream to stop me wrinkling and resembling a prune. When I had stowed it all in the car, which took three days, I drove off, hoping not to get lost en route. I've never been lost on foot and I've walked in places where no signposts exist. But I've never been known *not* to get lost when driving a car, despite maps and swotting up city plans in advance.

First I took the boat from Cork to Swansea. Then the motorway in a southerly direction. I had a slight attack of panic when a road sign north of Southampton read CALCUTTA and I thought, Oh no, I've done it again – I'm lost! The wind rose and I started to think of the crossing – 'a life on the ocean wave' and all that. When I finally passed through customs control and drove on to the ship, I was already feeling queasy, because I'd been looking at the swell from the dockside for over an hour in a force-ten gale.

I decided against dinner, as the ship and my stomach seemed to be undecided whether to rise up as far as heaven or descend into hell. Instead, I took to my bed and sang 'For Those in Peril on the Sea' and other hymns to perk up the morale. The stewardess brought me a cup of consommé and two Kwells. Having thanked her profusely, I staggered back to bed and lay hoping I'd be able to drive off in the morning and not be carried off on a stretcher like my nana when she went on the roughest crossing to the Isle of Man in thirty years.

The night was long and I vomited with great regularity, but finally I slept. I'd snored for about an hour when the stewardess reappeared with a pot of tea and a big smile.

'It's as calm as a millpond. The car passengers will be called in half an hour so don't go to sleep again.'

She handed me a tray with toast and marmalade and I ate and drank the whole potful. Then I went to clean my teeth and saw a pale eau-de-nil face looking at me from the mirror. I put on my largest pair of dark glasses and sat on the bed, tired and cross and uncertain of everything. If I were rich, I wouldn't buy jewels or spend house prices on couture clothes. I'd have a full-time chauffeur-handyman and a lady capable of keeping house and ironing everything, even collars. Finally I'd have a gardener to grow fruit and veg by the ton so I could live healthily and not get sick on boats. In the meantime, the prospect of a thousand miles of French motorway seemed like climbing Everest without oxygen and I didn't feel up to it.

The French customs officer asked me where I was going and I replied, 'To Provence'. He sighed, rolling his eyes in exasperation. 'Madame, you've taken a wrong turn. If you want to *leave* the docks you must turn right. This is the side for re-embarkation on the ship!' I turned right and drove in excess of the limit to the dock exit and then on to the open road.

An hour later, after numerous other wrong turns, I was on the motorway. The sky was leaden and fields on either side of the road were flooded. The landscape of Northern France is flat and not unlike Kent. Cows sit munching in fields, waiting for it to rain, and the houses are grey and square and squat. I sped on, anxious to be south of Paris and if possible at Beaune before exhaustion set in. I stopped for snacks, petrol and pipis but not for a midday meal in case of getting caught by the dreaded Demon Snoreloud. Finally, I put in to Mâcon, parked the car, took a room, and then, despite my exhaustion, emptied everything on to trolleys and pushed them inside to the safety of my room.

In the restaurant, where I hurried because I was famished by this time, I ate the entire dish of salade niçoise, given me by the waiter, unaware that it was a serving dish destined for three tables! Deprived fellow diners stared in amazement when I then wolfed down a filet of sole and a portion of green beans. The waiter scowled when I took only coffee. The French like four courses at least, including cheese and sweet. I like one or two and favour rice, pasta and fish as long as it has only one giant bone down the centre, as in turbot, halibut and baudroie. I was on my way out of the restaurant when I saw the figs, large purple figs, displayed with artistry in a wicker basket. I love figs and once ate two kilos, one after the other, bought from a lady who had just picked them from her garden in Nîmes. She had never before met anyone capable of eating two kilos of figs and said she would remember me for ever. I've not forgotten her, either, and often think of her old-world garden full of the scent of jasmine, coriander and cats.

Returning to my table, I asked the waiter to bring me some figs. He hurried away, relieved that I'd forgotten only to eat dessert. There were six in a small basket. I popped the first one in my mouth, bit into it and felt the explosion of seeds. They were quite perfect and I thought I'd eat six more. Then I had another coffee and went out for my after-dinner walk, using every bit of self-control not to order two kilos of those figs to be sent to my room.

In the cold night air I covered the length of the parking area and then crossed to the petrol station and back. I did this five times, pausing only to watch a deer in the distant field at the other side of the barrier fence. In the pale grey mist he seemed unreal and I wondered what he thought of the garish lights of the petrol station and the never-ending cacophony of cars on the motorway in what had once been a silent forest. There was an owl on the fence to my right and, a few yards further on, another, both sitting staring out like a couple who've had a row. Almost too tired to think, I returned to my room, took a shower, sprayed myself with perfume and watched five minutes of the late-night television news. My last thought was that I would surely sleep till midday. This is one of my favourite fantasies when tired.

In the morning, I woke at quarter to five, as usual. First I made tea on a machine in the suite. Then, still tired, I showered again before putting on the warpaint. At six, I ordered breakfast, my favourite meal of the day. The best British breakfasts are served in the most unlikely places, like the Raphael and Crillon Hotels in Paris, at brunch with champagne on Sunday in New York and in Scotland, where they give you venison sausages and all manner of oatmeal and medieval specialities that make you capable of tossing the caber or anything else for that matter. If I lived in Scotland, I'd have seven stomachs instead of the three that I already own.

In the dining room of the motorway hotel, I ate scrambled eggs and croissants with runny French jam. I prefer jam like we made every autumn in Ireland, with nothing but fruit, sugar and lemon juice. But the coffee was delicious and put me in a good mood, and, when I left the dining room to go to pay my bill, the waiter handed me a box with twelve perfect figs. 'I thought you'd be back for a third helping after dinner, madame, so I put these aside.' Frenchmen have many faults, as we all have, but they read female minds very well indeed.

I drove through Lyons and then past Valence, Montélimar and on towards Aix. The light was intense, but it was cold and I kept on my hat for travelling in Arctic conditions. I bought the hat at Inca, the Peruvian shop in London, and wear it only when my ears are at risk of freezing, because it gives me a definite 'one flew over the cuckoo's nest' look.

From Valence the scenery began to change and the savagery of the mistral became evident. Trees bent at acute angles towards the ground. Houses had inner courtyards and large gates to keep out the wind. I was fascinated by the pebble work set in concrete in geometric designs on the forecourt of old houses and shops. On main squares of off-motorway villages men stood outside the bars smiling and eyeing the passing scene. New arrivals in Provence are greeted with quizzical expressions. They take their time to assess you, deciding whether you're pretentious or not, honest or not, frank or a dissimulator. They're right: it takes a long time!

As I drove into the village I felt a sense of elation, almost of coming home, which was odd, because my home was in Southern Ireland. I was unpacking my things and carrying them from the car to the Bere house, when I saw Bébé pass by in a big beige car. On seeing me, he let out a loud miaow and tried to jump out of the window, but it was barely open. I was unaware that Bébé had been for a second visit to the vet and had escaped from his cat basket while Monsieur was driving home. I was so impatient to be with him that I hurried over to the house as soon as I'd carried my luggage upstairs and parked the car.

Bébé was sitting on the windowsill watching, waiting. I hurried to the boutique, borrowed a chair and climbed up to try to kiss him. The window was half closed, so I banged my nose hard, but it didn't matter. Unable to kiss Bébé, I slid my hand inside to the ledge where he was sitting, caressed his neck and told him how I'd missed him and how he was still the most beautiful cat in the world. Then, before returning to the house to unpack, I promised to pass by late on when he would be sitting on the roof taking the fresh night air.

When I had returned the chair to the boutique, I walked back to the Bere house, passing a white-haired man near Bébé's home. As he stood aside to let me pass by, he sneezed violently and I smothered a laugh, because my perfume contains incense and can provoke sensitive souls into comic spasms of atishoos.

At ten in the evening I walked through the silent village streets enjoying the scent of jasmine and honey-suckle. When I entered Bébé's street, I saw him sitting on the roof, outlined against a navy night sky. I called out, 'Goodnight, Bébé, see you in the morning.' And he miaowed, as if in reply, as he always had. Then he ran along the flat roof so he could miaow again when I turned to wave before disappearing from view.

In the morning, I went to the bar to drink my morning coffee. The white-haired man sneezed violently when I passed him by and Martine called out, 'That's a dangerous perfume you're wearing, Hélène.'

I took my place at table, sorted through the papers to be corrected and munched on my brioche aux raisins. Martine was leaning forward over the bar, listening to the white-haired man, and I wished I could hear what they were saying.

'You know, Martine, Bébé tried to jump out of my car yesterday afternoon.'

'Why on earth did he do that?'

'He saw the foreign lady and wanted to go to her. I can't understand it. He's twelve years old and he's never done such a thing before.'

'Don't worry about it. Hélène loves animals and Bébé senses that.'

'She *kisses* him and climbs on a chair so she can caress him, and yesterday she knocked her nose on my window but she didn't stop trying to get nearer to him!'

'She's in love with Bébé.'

'When she talks to him, Martine, I assure you that Bébé tries to reply. I'm sure they understand each other. *Mon Dieu*, what shall I do? My poor Bébé in love with a woman whose perfume makes everyone sneeze!'

When I'd read as much as I could understand of the local paper and done the first round of my writing corrections, I strolled to the stone house and stood under the window exchanging cat noises with Bébé. He joined in with enthusiasm, because this was one of our favourite games. When I made to leave, Bébé miaowed furiously, because I'd forgotten to stroke his neck. Then, as always, I returned the chair to the boutique and promised him I'd come by later. I was touched when Bébé extended his paw and touched my hand as I held it, for a moment, as near as I could to the sill. He was a remarkable cat and I loved him dearly. I walked home, wondering what to do for the best for the adorable animal.

Chapter Three

I decided to go to the beach for the whole day. First breakfast in a café overlooking the market at Sanary. Sunrise, in all its violet and fuchsia mystery, is at its most spectacular in the eastern Mediterranean. But sunrise in the south is unbeatable. First the sun appears reddish gold on the horizon. Then, slowly, it turns to rose. When the sea is calm, for a few precious moments, the colour of sea and sky fuse, giving the spectator the impression that the world is a sugar-pink skating rink stretching all the way to heaven. Then, slowly, before our eyes, the sky turns from peach to pale blue, darkening to that intense Mediterranean azure of a million picture postcards.

By ten thirty it was already hot. I checked my pages from the previous evening and decided to make my way to the promontory, where I imagined there might be fewer people. I was wrong, but I found a tiny space near two jolly Dutch girls and lay back to cook.

Five minutes later, I was surprised to receive a hard

knock on the right cheek and, looking up, saw an elderly man in long shorts jamming his viewfinder into my face. The Dutch girls told him to go away. I did too and he appeared to move a small distance away from me. I closed my eyes again and was almost asleep, when I felt someone astride my calves. It was the same man, this time accompanied by two others, all intent on photographing my anatomy, with as much touching as possible. I rose, dressed and walked back to my car, conscious that I had never much liked public beaches and would now avoid them.

I drove back to the village, disappointed about the beach, but not defeated. I would ask Martine if she knew anyone who had a house with a flat roof who might let me sunbathe there for an hour or two each afternoon. Perhaps it was a better idea. I would no longer have to lose my parking space on leaving the village each day and would be near my work in case of a sudden need to find a file or an important piece of documentation. I would be able to shower at home after sunbathing and go for my usual walk with Gastounet and Big Ears, to say nothing of being able to see the beautiful cat, as usual, morning and evening. There were lots of flat roofs in the village. I felt certain Martine would find one for me.

Having parked my car on the hill, I hurried to Martine's café. When I'd drunk a gallon of mineral water, I tried to explain what had happened on the beach and managed to ask if Martine could find anyone who might let me sunbathe on their roof. She listened, trying not to laugh at my murdering of the French language and promising to think about it. Then, to celebrate my talking French, as she put it with exemplary diplomacy, she offered me a glass of champagne. When the first glass was finished, I offered her a glass. Then I floated off to find Big Ears and Gastounet. It was time for our walk and we were all very fond of our routines.

The following morning, en route for breakfast in the café, I paused on the hill to look at a landscape that was clear in the minutest detail for miles around, because the icy mistral wind was blowing. For a few precious days, the heaviness of summer would be cleaned by the wind, which invigorated many and unnerved the more nervous visitors to the region.

I was correcting my pages when I became conscious of Martine pointing in my direction and a group of people at the bar laughing merrily. Glancing over to them I saw a pretty blonde with a tinkling voice, the village postman and the tall, white-haired man, who turned briefly to look in my direction. I finished my pages and returned to the house to ask Madame Bere if she knew anyone who might allow me to use their flat roof for an hour or two each afternoon. She was horrified.

'You can't sunbathe on a roof, Hélène! You'll be burned to a cinder.'

I tried to explain that I loved the heat, but Madame Bere was adamant.

'No! You might get ill with the heatstroke. Ask at one of the hotels in the region if you can swim and sunbathe there.'

Unwilling to go anywhere frequented by amateur photographers with protruding zoom lenses, I hurried upstairs to my apartment and set to work typing.

Three days later, Martine called me over when I'd

finished my work for the morning and handed me a key.

'One of my clients is willing to let you use his house in the afternoons. He's out for most of the day, every day. You don't have to pay. You just keep the key and make sure you double-lock the door when you leave. It's not far from your apartment. Madame Bere will show you where it is.'

At three o'clock I followed Madame Bere's instructions and found myself outside my favourite house. The beautiful cat was in the window looking down at me. Astonished by the coincidence, I just stood gazing up at the door without inserting the key. It was an old door of fine wood, studded like a castle entrance. Finally, I mounted the steps, inserted the key and stepped inside.

There was a kitchen to my left and one very large galleried room on my right. The room was full of books and prints of ancient aircraft, with a long refectory table in the centre. It was cool and airy and smelled of beeswax polish. Then I heard the cat jump down from the window in the kitchen and watched as he approached and stood very still, looking up at me in puzzlement. When I said his name, 'Hello, Bébé,' he seemed unable to believe that someone had entered his domain, that he was no longer alone.

I went upstairs, thinking Bébé would return to the kitchen once I disappeared to sunbathe. I was wrong. He followed a few paces behind me, through the winter garden full of leafy green shrubs and flowering cacti to the roof. The view was magnificent, the heat ovenlike, and I began to wonder if Madame Bere had been right in mocking my idea of a very private place to sunbathe. Bébé went downstairs to the winter garden and I could see him watching me from his own personal armchair.

Having put on lashings of sunscreen, I covered my hair with a cotton bandanna and lay down on my bath towel.

I managed ten minutes on the roof before deciding that if I stayed a minute longer I might indeed drop dead from heatstroke. Bébé was waiting patiently for me to come to my senses and we went down to the ground floor together. There, he climbed on to the table and began sniffing the basket I'd brought with me. It contained a slab of pâté de campagne for me to eat on the roof, as I hadn't had time for lunch. In the kitchen I found a plate and cut a slice of bread and there, near the window, Bébé and I ate our first meal together.

It turned out to be a memorable occasion, as Bébé ate as if he hadn't eaten for years. I managed two small mouthfuls before seeing the rest disappear in his direction. And all the while he purred and made gourmandising noises like a true Frenchman. When we'd finished, I washed my hands and the plate and put the remains in the paper bag into my basket. Bébé ran ahead of me to the living room and stood looking hopefully up as I approached the long sofa. Realising that he wanted affection and attention, I took him gently in my arms and lay down on the sofa. Outside, the sound of *cigales* filled the air. Inside, Bébé was purring so loud it was almost musical. After a while, we both slept.

I woke at four and thought I must finish my pages for the day. Stacking two big cushions behind my back, I wrote as Bébé slept on. When I had finished what had to be done, I knew it was time to go, but I didn't want to leave Bébé alone again. Finally I put my writing pad in the basket and gently lifted him on to a cushion. He sat up, looked at me and immediately leapt again on to my knee. Finally, I carried him to the kitchen, put him in his place at the window, kissed him a dozen times and promised to come again the following afternoon.

'Tomorrow, I'll cook a chicken and we'll eat it together. You'll like that, Bébé. All cats love chicken.'

When I'd locked the door, I reached up and touched his paw.

'See you again tomorrow Bébé.'

Madame Bere was waiting in the window, eyeing her watch and clucking like a mother hen.

'It's five o'clock. You didn't lie on the roof all this time, did you?'

'No, I only stayed on the roof for ten minutes. You were right: it's far too hot.'

'You've been with Bébé, haven't you? He'll be the happiest cat in the village tonight.'

'I'm going to take him a chicken tomorrow. We'll have a picnic in the living room. I hope the lady who owns him doesn't mind.'

'Bébé belongs to a gentleman.'

'The first name on the door is Jacqueline.'

'No, it says Jacquelin. That's the male version of Jacqueline. In France names can be masculine or feminine.'

'Well, I hope he doesn't mind if I keep his cat company. When we've had our picnic I shall write on the big sofa in the living room and let Bébé sleep on my lap.'

Madame Bere smiled a wise, secret smile and went about her work. I ran upstairs, wondering if I'd written well in the silent house, lying on the sofa with an affection-starved cat. When I read through the material, it was fine. I felt happier than I'd felt in ages.

Chapter Four

A friend came for breakfast in the bar. He ordered coffee and croissants while I sat in the wooden booth, hidden from sight because my usual table was full of tourists. We were discussing our work when I heard Martine talking about me to the tall, white-haired man who sneezed whenever I passed by. Intrigued by his curiosity, I listened to their conversation.

'Has the English lady said anything of her visits to my home?'

'Very little. I know she loves going because of Bébé, but I don't think she sunbathes any more. I always knew the roof would be too hot for her.'

'Of course, but if she doesn't sunbathe what does she do?'

'Madame Bere told me she cooks a chicken for Bébé almost every day and they eat together. Sometimes she buys chicken livers or duck pâté and they have a picnic in the kitchen. Then she writes with Bébé on her knee. Your house is much cooler in the afternoon than her apartment. Her side of the village takes the full blast of the afternoon sun.

'No doubt she has her own British logic, but I find the lady incomprehensible.'

For the first time Martine realised that Monsieur was suffering from conflicting emotions, exasperation, and anticipation in equal measures. His problem was that he couldn't stop thinking about the lady! Martine decided to be reassuring.

'Hélène's very happy with Bébé. She's lonely and so is he, so they've formed a friendship that seems to suit them both very well.'

My friend and I laughed delightedly at the French gentleman's astonishment. It was my pleasure to cook for Bébé and to eat with him and play with him and then write in Monsieur's cool living room. Now I'd identified Bébé's owner, I was certain he cared for his cat in a meticulous fashion. What he needed was a few lessons in how to excite Bébé's curiosity, his imagination and his desire to live his cat life to the full. I wondered whether Monsieur knew how to live life to the full or whether he was so precise and mathematical that he forgot the joy of a belly laugh, the golden pleasure of a moment shared.

The following day was the hottest in the region for a hundred years and far too hot for me, so, once Bébé and I had eaten, I took off my clothes and put on a filmy pareo of African cotton painted in tones of violet, orange and black. I put my shoes and clothes on the low table in the living room with my basket and then adjourned to the sofa with Bébé for a siesta. When I woke an hour later, I was thirsty and, having put Bébé on a cushion, went to the kitchen to take my bottle of mineral water out of the fridge. At that moment, Monsieur appeared, took one look at my near-naked state, turned puce and backed towards the door by which he'd just entered. I held out my hand and introduced myself.

'I'm Hélène Thornton. I'm sorry to be a bit short of clothes the first time we meet but it's so very hot.'

'I forgot my credit card. If you'll excuse me I'll go and get it and then leave you in peace.'

Returning to the sofa, I lifted Bébé back on to my stomach, picked up my writing pad and was working when Monsieur reappeared.

'Good afternoon to you, madame. Do please excuse me for surprising you.'

'I'm very happy to have met you, monsieur.'

When he had gone, I had a little smile at the puce shade Monsieur's face had assumed when he saw me. Bébé was still snoring happily and I gave him a kiss and whispered, 'Your master had quite a shock this afternoon. You must be especially nice to him this evening.'

Before leaving, I wrote Monsieur a note and left him the box of Leonidas chocolates I'd bought for him the previous day and a perfect tiny pine cone I'd found on my morning walk in the woods. I was very grateful for his kindness in letting me use his house and conscious that he and I were of different generations, different countries, different worlds. I wanted to be friendly but I wasn't quite certain how.

That evening, Martine was behind the bar at the café with her husband when Monsieur appeared. He was carrying a letter and looked unusually animated.

'I received this from the English lady. Can you translate it for me, Martine.'

She looked at the sepia ink and the forceful hand,

trying hard not to laugh at the unusual turn of phrase. She translated as if reading out loud . . . 'Dear Monsieur, I do hope you like chocolates. Thank you for letting me come to your home each day to see Bébé. Next time you arrive unexpectedly I hope to be fully dressed! I found this in the woods and thought you might like it. It's beautiful, isn't it? Beautiful and natural. My best, Hélène.'

Monsieur told Martine how he had succumbed to the temptation to eat all the delicious chocolates before dinner and then described the pine cone that he had placed next to his bed. A few minutes later, forgetting to pay for his wine, he walked slowly back to his house, folding the letter and putting it in his wallet to be kept in the secret compartment.

Martine glanced at her husband and they both smiled as she spoke.

'He doesn't realise it yet, but he's just been hit by a thunderbolt.'

Martine rang me immediately to tell me of Monsieur's visit and the fact that he was so affected by the letter that he'd forgotten to pay for his wine. She said that Monsieur had never forgotten to pay for his wine in all the years she had known him. It must be important, very important, she said. I replied that I would remember not to write him too many letters, and she laughed out loud.

By the end of the summer I was relaxed and tanned. I'd been in the region for a month and had been swimming each day. I'd written my chapters without too many problems and had slept well. By the end of September, the nights and early mornings turned cold. The sun still shone in the middle of the day, but I had to put blankets on my bed, one at the end of September and another in October. I was preparing for my autumn visit to the States and looking forward to it. Happy with the thought of new contracts and new challenges. I'd already packed my bags.

On Friday I got up, showered, said good morning to Lenny Lizard, who was on the point of hibernating and went to the market. As I was due to leave for the States, I didn't buy flowers. Instead, I chose lavender bags, potpourri and fruit. Feeling tired and a bit sick, I couldn't face my usual snack at the vendors' breakfast stall, so I drove back to the village, parking my car, now the season was over, as near to the house as possible.

Despite the icy wind, I was hot and sweating and when I switched off the ignition I was astonished to feel the sleeves of my silk blouse soaking wet, as were the rest of my clothes. For a few minutes I sat puzzling over this and trying to gather my strength. Then, picking up my basket, I opened the door, felt my knees buckle and slid down the side of the car, coming to rest on my backside. When I tried to get up, I couldn't, despite my will power and desire to do so. Shocked, I sat there, soaked to the skin with sweat, trembling all over and wondering what to do. I couldn't explain my collapse in French if anyone passed by and still couldn't get up. I closed my eyes, suddenly so ill I was hard pressed not to lie down and cry.

When I opened my eyes, I saw two feet next to mine and travelling upwards recognised Bébé's owner. He held out his hand to help me up and I tried, but my legs wouldn't move. The pain between my ribs at the apex of the stomach was so intense I could barely speak. I managed just three words: 'I am ill.' Then I watched through a haze of pain as Monsieur called a mason to help him carry me back to the apartment. Another resident offered to park my car on the hill and a young girl carried my market purchases, hurrying ahead and ringing the bell at the Bere house.

I lay back, trying hard not to give way to tears from pain and shock. Then across the room, I saw Monsieur's face as he stood looking in seeming disbelief at the objects of my daily life. There was a hand painted silk kimono hanging over the chair and my big, black type-writer on the table. The apartment smelled of lilies and musk and the chicken I'd cooked for Bébé before going out.

I watched Monsieur step nearer the coffee table to get a better look at the Gogol novel, the pot of basil, the pine cones and beach pebbles. He didn't touch anything because he was too well mannered to do so. Then he saw the poem and I smiled as curiosity overcame him and he extended a long, slim hand so he could read the translation of a quatrain by Ikago no Atsuyuki, the tenth century Japanese poet: 'My great regret is that I cannot divide myself in two. But my invisible heart will follow you everywhere.'

I enjoyed the brief lapse in Monsieur's perfection, provoked by his curiosity of the unknown. It made him seem very human and I liked that. I liked it a lot.

The doctor said I had to have tests the following morning and I heard Monsieur agreeing to drive me to the specialist concerned. Then, having told me to try to sleep, he went downstairs to reassure the Beres. I closed my eyes and tried not to let panic enter on stage. I was in a country where I barely spoke the language and was suffering from a potentially difficult illness. Instinct told me that something was complicating my condition, but I couldn't work out what it could be and the uncertainty worried me to death.

Madame Bere was relieved that Monsieur had taken charge with such efficiency. She was surprised when he returned eleven times before nightfall to check that her lodger was no worse. She had taken tea, a bottle of water and a bowl of consommé upstairs, worried by the lady's grey pallor and obvious pain. She would surely not be able to leave for New York in two weeks' time as she had planned. Madame decided not to relet the apartment, hoping secretly that her lodger would stay on.

At eight the next morning Monsieur helped the sick woman into his car and drove off at his usual sedate pace. Madame Bere watched from behind the jasmine-framed window, noting that Monsieur was dressed for a special occasion. Turning to her husband, she remarked, 'He is in love but he doesn't realise it.'

'Don't talk nonsense!'

'You'll see. They are as different as two people can be, but I wouldn't be surprised if . . .'

Madame Bere cleared the breakfast things and thought how the couple had met because of the lady's passion for Bébé the beautiful cat. She peeled potatoes and vegetables for *soupe au pistou*, made with fresh basil and her own secret thickener. She decided to make enough for four, in case Monsieur decided to stay for lunch.

After several incomprehensible examinations, the specialist informed Monsieur that I had gallstones as big as the rock of Gibraltar and that I must have had them for years. I agreed, saying that I'd been suffering pain for ten years but had never been diagnosed. The specialist looked to Monsieur and said, '*C'est pas vrai!*' When I said I was leaving for the States in less than two weeks, he and Monsieur looked appalled and I, thinking to comfort them, said, 'Don't worry, I shall eat very little in New York, just toast and fruit.' At this Monsieur rolled his eyes in horror. 'Toast and fruit! You'll be dead in a week. I should accompany you, but I once ate a famous hamburger from America and I decided not to eat their food again. It was served without a knife and fork and the ketchup fell on my trousers!'

I asked to be taken home, exhausted by the tests and put out by Monsieur's passion for eating. I was unaware at the time that, to a Frenchman, a woman who doesn't show an interest in eating has to be looked after, taught and protected from her ignorance of one of the great pleasures of life.

Monsieur stayed with me for a long time, sitting at the far end of the room with a book, while I lay on my bed trying to pretend I was well again. Before leaving the house, Monsieur said, 'I shall drive you to Nice Airport for your flight to New York. The Pan American flight comes from Rome and is the one that terrorists exploded last week. Security will be very long, so tell your friends in New York that you will arrive at Kennedy Airport later than usual.'

To take my mind off my condition, Monsieur invited me to lunch a few days later. He talked of his childhood in the *département* of Lorraine, of the cold, windy climate, the love of good, heavy food like giant stews, sausages and bacon and big tarts of all dimensions. It sounded just like the north of England, where I was partly raised, and I drew his attention to the similarities. He talked then of his love of flying and his passion for the history of aviation. I tried not to show that in my view anything resembling a plane should be coated with icing and preserved in a museum, but never allowed to take off. I told him about my favourite areas of the world, especially the East Coast of the USA. I described the duck pond in East Hampton, the red barns of Vermont and the autumn spectacle of the New England region. There were long pauses for me to search for words in my *Collins Robert Dictionary* and once or twice I had to draw things for him. When I drew Bébé he immediately took the picture to be framed.

Monsieur insisted on driving me everywhere, in case I should be taken ill again. As I dislike driving and Monsieur loves it, this suited me fine and, without realising it, we drew closer and closer together. Soon we had private jokes, usually based on my unacceptable frankness and lack of understanding of diplomacy. Monsieur pronounced me the most honest woman in the world and the one most likely to start World War Three if ever elected to government.

Monsieur mentioned one day that he had had an alsatian dog when he first arrived in the region. His passion for cats had only begun, he told me, at the age of 53, after Bébé had tutored him in the art of cat-manship. I was surprised, because I believe there are cat people and dog people and 'rarely the twain shall meet'.

It was a beautiful day, so we went for a walk, 'to help your liver to be well', as Monsieur put it. I carried my dictionary and we talked about everything under the sun. We were getting to know each other with surprising speed and 'forming liens', as Saint-Exupéry said. Then, at the end of the walk, something odd happened that seemed to cement the dawning conspiracy between us.

She was a slim, rather haggard-looking woman with iron-grey hair, beautiful blue eyes and a haughty manner. Known for her love of very large dogs and even larger men, she paused outside the house eyeing Bébé, who was sitting, as usual, on the sill. Then she turned to Monsieur.

'Does your cat bite?'

Monsieur's eyebrows shot up and he looked to see if the lady was being unpleasant.

'Dogs bite, madame. Cats rarely do.'

'Does he scratch?'

'Rarely, and only by accident.'

'Does he have worms?'

I watched Monsieur rise up to his full height, take out his door key and disappear from view. Feeling the question deserved a suitable response, I struggled to find the correct words.

'Bébé has thousands of worms. We eat them for breakfast, on toast, with lots of Gentleman's Relish.'

The lady blinked three or four times and then moved on, stunned, no doubt, by the horrible image. I was unaware at the time that the French sense of humour bears no relation whatsoever to the English one, because they take everything literally.

Monsieur was delighted, in fact joyful. He produced a bottle of champagne, telling me the magnesium and potassium in it were 'good for the liver'. Then, looking at me out of the corner of his eye, he said, 'I invite you to come for breakfast. We shall have worms on toast and coffee.'

'I'll come at eight fifteen.'

And he patted my hand and smiled a secret smile, happy as a king.

Madame Bere was thrilled by all this and spent a great

deal of time with her nose glued to the window in case 'Monsieur' should appear. She had done her best to find out all about him and recited what she knew of his life and character, as if they were old friends. One of the differences between the French and British is the Gallic enthusiasm for the '*coup de foudre*' – love at first sight. The British find it hard to believe in love at short notice and Madame's romantic notions quite amazed me. Still, she repeated frequently, 'Monsieur is in love. He will make a proposal of marriage very soon.'

And I stomped off to bed, furious with all the talk of hearts and flowers and worried to death in case my insurance for New York might be insufficient if my gallstones decided to start moving.

Chapter Five

A few days before my departure for the States, I was taken ill with spasms of pain and again confined to bed. Monsieur visited, his face ashen pale. Madame Bere had made a wonderful vegetable soup and Monsieur stayed for lunch and ate two helpings of everything. I ate half a bowl to show my appreciation, but all I really wanted to do was go to bed for an hour before hurrying away to see Bébé. At two o'clock Monsieur left, saying he would return to see me in the evening and I walked, accompanied by Madame Bere, to his house to deliver the chicken to Bébé, listening in silence as Madame protested that I should have stayed in bed.

I felt better the moment I saw Bébé and when he had eaten we slept on the sofa for the rest of the afternoon. I didn't write a word, just lay there at peace with the world, trying to pretend I wasn't ill. Then I gave Bébé a double ration of kisses and walked round the corner to the apartment. I'd just had a shower and was reading in bed, when Monsieur arrived, his face full of exasperation.

'Madame Hélène, have you been out?'

'Yes, of course. I took Bébé his chicken lunch like always.'

'But you are ill, you must stay in bed.'

'As long as I can walk there's no excuse for disappointing Bébé. It's only fifty yards to your house and I look forward to seeing him.'

'I never heard such nonsense!'

'It's not nonsense. Bébé waits for me at around two each day. I leave at five. Your cat is the loneliest pet I ever met. He needs love and kisses and personal attention, not croquettes measured on a letter scale! Why do you leave him alone all day? Why can't you take him with you from time to time? And have you thought how lonely he's going to be when I leave in two weeks' time? Well? Say something!'

Monsieur seemed nonplussed and his lack of response made me angry. Forgetting that I was ill, I leapt out of bed, more furious by the minute because I didn't have enough words in French to berate him. At that moment, Monsieur put on his highly logical look and spoke very softly, as if trying to calm a wildcat.

'You cannot leave because you are ill. You will have to stay on. Leaving is impossible.'

My nana taught me that nothing is impossible, so I stood up as straight as the pain would allow and said defiantly, 'Impossible is not a word in my dictionary.'

'*Mon Dieu!* You could make a saint angry!'

Thoroughly unhappy and worn out, I flopped down on the bed.

'I'm tired. I want to go to sleep.'

'I'm sorry. I shall drive you to the airport if you insist

on going to New York, but think very hard, because if you are ill in that city it will be awful. I'll come in the morning to see how you are.'

'Thank you for all you've done for me today. Give Bébé a big goodnight kiss from Hélène.'

Suddenly, I felt empty and frightened. I had work commitments I was no longer sure I could fulfil. The doctors had said an operation within three months was the only way to avoid a dangerous emergency situation. I had replied 'no hospitals', but the reality of my situation was fast dawning on me. Looking towards Monsieur, I saw concern and something else: an awareness of my insecurity and the fact that I was afraid because I was balanced on the edge of a precipice. He said 'goodnight' very softly and walked out of the room. If I could have run after him to apologise for my outburst I would have done, but all the strength had gone from me.

Madame Bere opened the door and invited Monsieur in for a glass of wine.

'How do you find Hélène?'

'She is surely the most obstinate person in the world and I exasperated her so much she leapt out of bed and growled like a tiger every time she couldn't find the words with which to tell me off.'

Madame Bere laughed out loud.

'If she's like that when she's ill, you can imagine how she is when she's well! My husband thinks you'd best remember the rules of big-game hunting: keep calm, keep cool and keep your distance in case of sudden confrontations.'

*

I woke at three and couldn't sleep again. In the hours of night, problems seem twice as big and ten times as ominous as in the daytime. For some time I'd been feeling lousy, working too hard, too long and never looking after myself. Like the little dancer who danced till she died, I'd continued at a breakneck pace because work was my panacea. But now, what should I do? The doctors had ordered an operation within three months or catastrophe. If I was ill and couldn't work, I also faced losing my precious independence. When we're well, we put the possibility of ever being ill to the back of our minds. Then, when it happens, we don't know what to do.

At four I made tea and sat watching the sunrise over the distant sea. Should I extend my stay so I could leave from Nice instead of doing the exhausting drive home before my departure? I decided Monsieur was right. It would be best to stay on for a short while. When Madame Bere had had breakfast, I would go and ask if I could extend by a month until the end of October. Decision made, I went back to bed.

In the small hours before dawn, I thought of Monsieur and how he had eyed the low table full of my favourite things. I couldn't resist a smile as I tried to imagine him reading Gogol. The Russian's oblique view of everything would probably irritate a man as straightforward as Monsieur. He seemed to like natural things, so the pine cones had pleased him. How, I wondered, had he reacted to the poem that contained the passionate lines of Atsuyuki? From a bourgeois family in the east of France, Monsieur appeared outwardly calm and unmoved by the turbulent events of each day. I suspected, however, that passion was not alien to his nature. I had seen it when he talked of planes and flying them. I wondered then if he had remembered to kiss Bébé on his return home, as I'd asked him to. And had he sneezed, because his cat was always rubbing against the perfumed region of my throat?

In the morning, I went to see Madame Bere to ask if I could keep the apartment for an extra month. She agreed at once and offered me breakfast. As I drank my coffee, I remembered that Monsieur had said he listened to the French naval weather forecast each morning at six fifty-five. When I had finished my coffee, I ran upstairs and put on the radio, but didn't understand much of the French naval weather forecast. Still, having made the decision to stay on, I was relieved and more settled. Within minutes I was in bed and sound asleep.

When I woke finally, I felt a bit conscience-stricken that I had shown a certain displeasure before Monsieur the previous evening and had berated him for feeding Bébé nothing but croquettes. He had been so very kind and I had been exasperated because I was in pain. I remembered then that the local paper had shown the publicity for a film about early pioneers in the world of aviation. Picking up the phone, I called Monsieur and invited him to come over to watch it that evening. He accepted immediately and arrived ten minutes later with a bottle of champagne, 'in case we get thirsty during the evening'.

I got out my encyclopedia and swotted up a few facts on the fliers who were the subject of the film. In the afternoon, Madame Bere delivered home-made canapés in case Monsieur got hungry. In France, the evening news is at eight and the film follows at eight thirty. Monsieur arrived at seven thirty, opened the champagne, ate all the canapés, as I couldn't touch them, watched the evening news intently and then, when the opening titles of the film began to roll, proceeded to snore softly, with alarming precision. At ten thirty, as the end credits appeared, Monsieur woke, prompt on cue and said, 'It was an excellent film, wasn't it?'

It took many a long month for Monsieur to admit that he disliked the cinema, films and in particular films on television. He had therefore perfected the technique of falling asleep at the beginning and waking at the end. I was impressed!

The following morning as house clocks struck ten, the telephone rang. Madame Bere answered the call, listened, said yes half a dozen times and then ran off, singing joyfully, to tell her husband the news.

'Monsieur rang and when I told him Hélène had asked to stay on for another month, he said to keep the apartment free till the end of the year and he'll guarantee payment. I tell you he's in love. They'll get married in the spring, you'll see.'

'I forbid you to discuss all this. You're having romantic fantasies that are not based on fact.'

'Indeed they are! He's a very dear, kind man and she's lonely and ill and needs him. That's a good base for the start of a romance if ever I heard one.'

Madame hurried away to make soup, which was all her lodger dared eat apart from bread. She would also make a fig tart in case Monsieur decided to stay for lunch again. Happy as a lark, she sang as she worked. Who would have thought an English lady of wilful nature would attract someone like Monsieur? She laughed joyfully as she thought of the gentleman who was so polite that he was taken aback and knocked senseless every ten minutes by the brutal directness of the invalid. Madame was confident that soon Monsieur would show a surprising turn of speed and decision that would enchant her lodger.

Every afternoon, I went to see Bébé, needing the routine to convince myself that I was well again and looking forward to his affection, because being ill had made me vulnerable. On the day before my departure for New York, I lay on the sofa, thinking of Monsieur. He was a very well-organised person with a predictable life. He liked doing the household accounts, going on his boat and measuring things with precision. He also liked remembering his days as a flying instructor, his passion for planes as intense as my detestation of them. I often smiled at the memory of the day when I had told him how I hated flying. Taken aback by such an aberration, he had protested, 'But Hélène, a plane is an object of wonder and the safest way to travel.'

'I don't like it at all. I do it, because I must, but I'm ill at ease if my feet aren't firmly planted on the ground.'

'Do you like sailing?'

'I was born near the sea and I've always loved it and I like watching boats – from afar. But if the sea's rough I get sick just standing on the quayside looking out.'

'Impossible! I never heard of such a thing.'

'I assure you it's true.'

Monsieur had tried hard to find some common ground for conversation, without success. Our only common ground was a love of cats and our need for the orderly life. Monsieur adored eating. I thought of it as an unfortunate necessity. Monsieur liked sailing, planes, mathematics and fiddling with the interior of his car. I couldn't add two and two together, broke every machine I ever tried to use and planes and boats made me weep. I liked reading, painting, writing, collecting stones on the beach and renovating old houses. Monsieur detested perfumes. I collected them. But we both loved Bébé, the most beautiful cat in the world.

Despite our immense difference of character, Monsieur was a delightful companion, relating stories of his family and of railway stations that he knew would interest me because of my passion for trains. Often I thought of the station in Metz, where Monsieur had told me the corridors leading to the platforms had been constructed wide enough to 'permit an army to pass.' My favourite stories, however, concerned La Tante Marthe, Monsieur's aunt, who lived near Saint-Tropez. She had been a great beauty in her youth and a dazzling, avant-garde personality. She had driven a Delage, when few women drove, and had been dressed by Chanel, wowing the most eligible men in Paris before marrying the gentleman of her choice. Now 84, she was waiting for a visit from her nephew. Seeing my interest in her subject, Monsieur had invited me to meet his aunt on my return from America and I'd accepted.

When I thought of the trip to New York, I felt my confidence ebbing. I had to go, but would my weak condition stand up to the rigors of two weeks of business meetings? My uncertainty about the situation increased daily, until Monsieur arrived to pick me up and take me to the airport.

'Is the shoulder bag all the luggage you're taking, Hélène?'

'I can't carry anything heavy, so I've packed clothes that I can roll in a ball.'

'Very wise. I'll drive you first to the house so you can give Bébé his chicken. Then we'll leave.'

I prepared Bébé's chicken for the last time for two weeks. The thought of not seeing him upset me, so I told Bébé that I was going away for a little while but that I would be back. Bébé looked into my eyes as if he understood every word and I had to hold back my tears. I don't like crying in front of people, so I stood there, blowing my nose and trying to stay in control. When I'd kissed Bébé a dozen times and then another dozen times, I walked out to the car and stood waiting for Monsieur to unlock it. I was so upset to be leaving, I almost cancelled the trip. Monsieur looked hard into my eyes, as if aware of every thought. Then, without a word, he drove us on to the motorway towards Nice.

Before I passed through the barrier, Monsieur handed me a letter.

'I've written my private number on a paper with one or two other things. Read it when you get on the plane.'

'I don't know what I'd have done without you these last two weeks,' I told him.

'I shall be here to meet you when you return. And don't forget what I told you: if you start feeling unwell again, change your ticket and come back at once.'

With great tenderness, I put my arms around his neck and kissed his cheeks.

'Thank you again for everything.'

Monsieur blushed turkey red, which pleased me no end. Before disappearing into the departure lounge, I turned and waved. He was still there, standing quite still, and I remember thinking that, with his sense of responsibility and his fear of my being ill, he was prob-ably wondering whether to buy a ticket and accompany me, in case I needed him. The only thing that would stop him would be his terror of American food and giant New York portions. Monsieur liked elegance and style. A foot-long plate of ice cream would send him into a decline. The thought made me smile and I realised for the first time that he had become part of the daily routines of my life.

Monsieur walked slowly back to the car park and drove to the outskirts of the airport to watch the plane. The separation would be difficult for Bébé and, he had to admit, for him. He had grown accustomed to her despite her incapacity to add up her chequebook counterfoils each week and her habit of turning on the coffee machine before putting in the water. He thought of the softness of her skin when she had kissed him and realised that for once he had not sneezed because of her perfume. He was making progress. And so was she!

There was a security check at passport control, then another just before we got on the bus to go to the plane. On entering the plane, when everyone thought the searches were over, officers of an elite squad went through everyone and everything again. Finally, we took off and I clutched the seat arms till my knuckles showed white. All I wanted at that moment was to return home. It came as something of a shock to me to realise that 'home' was synonymous with the living room of Monsieur's house, the sofa and Bébé on my knee. It was also Monsieur making coffee on his antiquity of a machine and just being there, an ever-watchful but precious presence. Closing my eyes I tried to concentrate on New York, but my disobedient brain returned again and again to a stone house and a gentleman I barely knew.

Chapter Six

It was after my return from America that I found the note Monsieur had given me at Nice Airport. Crumpled in a corner of my shoulder bag, it had remained unopened during my travels. Having poured myself a cup of tea, I tore open the envelope and read . . .

My telephone number is 49 51 68 78.
 If you feel ill, please return immediately.
 I would like to say that when you come back I shall propose marriage. Bébé and I do not wish to lose you, ever.

Amazed, I sat for a long time thinking. Imagine such a reticent man writing such a letter! Work was put aside while I rolled the unexpected proposal around in my head. Then, needing my familiar routines, I went to the café for the morning coffee and sat looking at the flames leaping up the chimney and forgetting to correct my pages. Monsieur had neither mentioned the note nor asked for a response. I knew him well enough now to realise that he would wait for the perfect moment to put the question face to face. For twenty years I'd avoided all possibility of remarrying. As I walked slowly back to my apartment, I wondered what I really wanted and why.

The following morning we drove to Saint-Tropez to lunch with La Tante Marthe. The journey was comfortable, the autumn weather perfect, and we passed through hills covered in heather and a dense forest that led to the resort. Now and then we saw a wild pig running among the cork oaks and everywhere there was the smoky smell of late autumn, the mellow pungency of mushrooms, fruit and bonfires.

On arrival, I looked up at the house, which was pure, picture-book Provence, its ancient walls a faded bois de rose, its shutters dark green. The garden was a fairy-tale place of bowers and pergolas laden so heavily with flowers they seemed to lean for support on the walls of the house.

In advanced old age, Tante Marthe had put all her energy into helping raise funds for a chapel in the domain where she lived. I was therefore expecting to meet a white-haired, venerable French matron of forbidding personality. Instead, I watched a reed-slim pretty woman in a mauve Chanel suit run down the stone steps to welcome us. Then she ran back to the house to find her housekeeper and members of the family who'd come to meet me. Bewildered, I turned to Monsieur.

'Is that Tante Marthe's companion?'

'No, Hélène, that is Tante Marthe.'

I entered the house open-mouthed in astonishment and came face to face with a handsome grey parrot, the arch villain Jacquot, who turned visitors pale with a vocabulary of swearwords in four languages and a wicked character that turned sunny only for Tante Marthe. Unaware of his reputation, I chatted to the parrot, who did his 'amiable Jacquot' act, till I made the error of trying to scratch his head through the cage bars. At this point, he bit me hard and I, hurt and furious, shouted, 'Bad boy Jacquot, horrible bad boy.'

I was trying to eat one of those impossible, wobbling French desserts, when Jacquot burst out with 'Bad boy, Jacquot. Bugger off, bugger off.'

After lunch, Tante Marthe showed me the garden, with its acres of mimosa, eucalyptus and climbing plants brought from all over the world by her late husband. We spent a long time in the hothouse, full of orchids and scented fronds of jasmine. And all around there were roses in bloom, witness to the mildness of that region.

When it was time to leave, Tante Marthe walked with us to the car, kissed us both and stood on the steps waving. I sat in silence, trying to work out how she'd stayed so young and gay and modern. There were many astonishing characters in Monsieur's family, some of them present that day, but Tante Marthe was the queen of them all.

Monsieur was in a rare good humour on arrival in the village and we ate dinner in a little restaurant near my apartment. At the end of the meal, he proposed and I expressed my uncertainty about the idea.

'I've avoided thinking of remarrying for twenty years.'

'Well, you can't avoid it any longer, because I intend to marry you. But take your time. Bébé and I have a lot of patience and the tenacity of two Dobermans.'

At the door of the Bere house, Monsieur kissed me

on both cheeks and then turned towards his own home. I watched him go, my mind racing in ever-increasing uncertainty. Then I went upstairs and found a note from Madame Bere on the table.

'Please telephone your friend Fiona in Ireland,' it read.

When I finally got through, I was informed that there'd been a burglary at my rented house near Galway. Could I return for a few days to sort things out and make the necessary insurance claims? I telephoned Monsieur and told him the news and he, calm as always, said, 'I will drive you to Marseilles Airport tomorrow morning. There is a flight to London at ten thirty.'

I had wanted to go home, but suddenly I realised that I didn't want to leave Monsieur. All these conflicting emotions made it impossible to sleep and I was still trying to identify my feelings, while eating chicken soup at midnight. I was looking out into the moonlit country-side, when the phone rang and Monsieur spoke.

'Why are you not asleep?'

'I'm thinking. How did you know I wasn't asleep?'

'Because I can't sleep either, so I went to walk in the car park near your apartment and I saw the light and wondered if you were ill again.'

'I'm trying to work out why I'm sad to be leaving.'

There was a pause before he spoke.

'I shall tell you why when you return from Ireland. You won't need more than a few days there. Then you'll be here for Christmas and we'll have a real French fête.'

The following morning I was in the cockpit with the BA crew. I didn't look at the knobs and instruments so adored by Monsieur. Instead, I gazed in wonder at the clouds and the colours in a world that seemed made of meringue. I remember it as the nearest thing I ever saw to my idea of the pathway to heaven. After returning to my seat, I wrote down my feelings at this unimagined beauty and, translating it into very bad French, put it on a card to be sent to Monsieur.

On that first evening back in Ireland my hard-drinking neighbour came with his dogs to offer consolation. He had a bottle of champagne in the fridge and his sister had cooked a 'to hell with burglars' celebration dinner. After the meal, he regaled us all with stories of the Sudan, gin-drinking competitions with fellow agricultural experts and some quite astounding accounts of native uses for dung. He'd remained there for 25 years, a wonderful human advert for Gordon's Gin, laughing too much and being one of nature's great gentlemen.

On the fourth morning of my stay, I received a letter from Monsieur . . .

Bébé and I are lonely. We are waiting to hear the time and date of your arrival in Marseilles. I shall be at the airport to meet you and am trying hard to control my desire to go there immediately in case of a miracle!

This note made me realise why I hadn't wanted to leave France. Like so many bad happenings in life, the burglary had had positive effects too, forcing me to admit that, after resisting remarriage for over twenty years, I was coming round to the idea.

The first thing I did on my return was run around the corner to see Bébé. He was in the window, watching, as always, and as I entered the house we had a joyful reunion. Bébé went immediately to inspect my basket, to check that I'd brought a tasty something for him.

Then he ran to the sofa and leapt on my chest as I lay stretched out at his side. Exhausted after the long journey, I slept immediately, waking only when Monsieur appeared to announce that his housekeeper had made lunch. First I gave Bébé his chicken. Then I sat facing Monsieur for our first meal in his home. I was surprised when he continued to watch his cat eating in the kitchen. Bébé was showing his usual yum-yum appreciation.

'Does Bébé always make those noises when you feed him?'

'Almost always. He loves chicken livers and pâté de campagne.'

'I give him croquettes.'

'They're fine every other day, but he gets bored with them. All that crunching's a bit of a nuisance. Imagine if you had to eat nothing but croquettes.'

Monsieur swallowed hard, watching as Bébé took his place on the sofa to wait for the lady's return. Hélène appeared to be unaware of the upheaval she had caused in his life, to say nothing of the earthquake that had happened in Bébé's mundane existence. He wondered if she would give him an answer to his proposal of marriage and how to crystallise her thoughts so she would accept. He decided to leave it to Bébé.

During my absence, Monsieur had ordered crates of champagne, so he could invite me for an aperitif and then, if I was free, to dinner. He was exhausted by the stress of staying at home waiting for me to call from Ireland so he could come and meet me at the airport. I was a bit exhausted too and had to have a quick snooze on the sofa with Bébé, who purred loud and long, protesting when I finally rose to leave. Kissing his head and rubbing my cheek against his ears, I lifted him on to his cushion on the sofa.

'I have to go and finish my pages, Bébé, but I'll be back.'

He touched my hand gently with his paw and I bent to kiss him again.

'Soon I shan't be leaving any more and you'll be able to sit on my bed when I write . . .'

Hearing this, Monsieur leapt up as if he'd had an electric shock.

'Would Saint-Tropez in the spring be a good idea for the wedding, Hélène? Does the idea please you?

'Sounds perfect to me.'

Bébé was gazing up at Monsieur with great intensity. When his master flopped down in the armchair, Bébé leapt up on to his knee and looked eagerly into his eyes, as if he had understood every word of our conversation. Monsieur was stroking him absent-mindedly when I let myself out of the house. I would return later and we'd talk, but for the moment Monsieur needed time to recover from his emotions.

Monsieur whispered to his cat.

'She said yes Bébé. You and I will have to be perfect so she won't change her mind before the spring. You're responsible for all this, you know. She'd never have noticed me, but she loved you from the very first day. What a basis for a marriage! I shall ask myself to the end of my days if she married me or my cat.'

Bébé snuggled up to his master. Soon, they would never be alone again and all because of the lady. In his innocent way, Bébé loved her with deep devotion and he always would.

*

Before starting work, I went to pick up Big Ears for our afternoon walk together. I'd brought her some chicken leftovers from lunch and enjoyed watching as she relished the treat. I was very conscious that if it hadn't been for Big Ears Monsieur might never have noticed me. Fate was strange and suddenly life seemed like a kaleidoscope, ever changing ever surprising, with daily events falling into place like pieces in a puzzle.

Big Ears and I ended our tour at the candle shop, so she could see her new suitor, a handsome grey tomcat with a head like Caesar. Before returning to work, I picked Big Ears up and stroked her ears so she would know that I would never neglect her, despite Bébé's presence in my life.

Monsieur was searching for his cat but Bébé was nowhere to be found. Then, when he entered the tiny guest bedroom where Hélène had left some belongings brought back from Ireland, he found Bébé fast asleep on an embroidered pillow. Monsieur sighed, because his cat was forbidden to lie on beds. He was also forbidden to lie on the sofa, but Hélène had changed all that.

Monsieur tried to work out what she would think of Bébé on her bed and decided that she would say that what was hers was also his. Looking down at the cat, Monsieur was overcome by a wave of tenderness. Bébé had never been happier and neither had he.

That night, alone in my little apartment, I lay awake, invaded by a sense of unreality. I was going to get married. It didn't seem possible that after almost twenty years of saying no to proposals I had changed my mind. When I tried to work out why this had happened I couldn't find a reason. All I knew was that all the decades of incessant travel were over. I wanted and needed to settle down and put down real roots. Above all, I didn't want to leave Monsieur and Bébé and our way of being together. I tossed and turned all night, half afraid of the changes to come, half excited by the possibility of a new beginning.

Chapter Seven

The wedding should have been a morose affair, as it rained like the Indian Monsoon, flooding streets and reducing the dazzling light of Provence to a sullen iron grey. Tante Marthe, exquisite in lilac, ignored the weather and even a torrent that came down the hill and soaked everyone's feet and legs to the knees. The table was festive, the food delicious and Jacquot the parrot was on his best and most appalling form, shouting 'Bugger off!' and other encouragements of a forbidden nature throughout the meal.

One guest played the piano. Staff brought champagne and a surprise cake. It was all perfect, the only cloud on the horizon being my exhaustion and the fact that I felt as sick as when I'd been ill. For the moment I tried unsuccessfully not to think of bad health and listened to the toasts. It was all over too soon and as I ran to the car to avoid another deluge, I was happy and so was Monsieur.

We arrived home still covered in rose petals and confetti. Bébé was at the window miaowing a welcome, and some of the neighbours came and shook hands and wished us well. A feeling of incredulity at being married gave way to the pleasure of being in the now familiar house. Having fed Bébé and spoiled him to death, we settled in to an evening of music and making plans.

After a certain time, Monsieur asked, 'Where is Bébé?'

'Perhaps he went to the roof.'

'He never goes up at this time.'

'He could have changed his habits.'

When it was time to sleep, Monsieur was still searching for his cat. I went to my room and sat on the bed wondering how I could transport all my books from my former home and where to put them. There was no storage space in this tiny bedroom and the property I had bought on my first visit to the area needed months of work. I'd bought it cheap because the odour of cat pee-pee was so strong that potential buyers had avoided the possibility of extended viewing of the property. I was mulling over all this when I realised that Bébé was asleep on the pillow next to mine. Seeing him there looking so happy made me happy too and I stroked his silky back until he purred.

It occurred to me that a wedding night spent with a cat was rather an odd idea. Unsettled by all the excitement, I went up to the flat roof and there, outlined against the night sky, was Monsieur. I slid under his arm and he told me his thoughts.

'Bébé is an unbeatable rival, I'm afraid.'

'Why don't I bring the mattress from the winter garden so we can lie under the stars and talk.'

'Impossible! Someone might see us – and anyway it's getting cold.'

'I don't mind being seen by a seagull and we won't stay long.'

I lugged a day-bed mattress from the adjacent winter garden and lay down under the stars. Monsieur was visibly wrestling with convention, but eventually joined me. And in the still of night he achieved perfect take-off. Choosing my words carefully and knowing his passion for aviation, I whispered, 'I didn't expect you to be supersonic.' Monsieur savoured the compliment, repeating it to himself a couple of times. Then, arm in arm, we went downstairs, he to his room, where he fell immediately asleep, I to mine, where I lay wide awake and full of energy, wishing it was four in the morning, so I could get up and have coffee.

Bébé opened his eyes and I knew he was wondering if I would put him out because he was forbidden to lie on beds. Unable to resist the appeal in his eyes, I told him about the fat chicken I was going to buy for his lunch the next day. Bébé crept forward till his head was on my shoulder and within seconds we were both asleep.

Those first weeks of marriage were dangerous because Monsieur's politeness stopped him saying anything directly critical. I had become totally vegetarian, adoring food steamed, simmered and spicy. Monsieur likes steak and fried potatoes, pizzas, roast pork and anything cooked in olive oil. He hates everything simmered or stewed and thinks all vegetables are to be eaten 'another day', with the exception of potatoes, which he adores – fried. He therefore suffered in silence from my dietary ideas. When I found out, I threw a Callas volume rage. Monsieur reacted with astonishment that a British person could shout like an Italian

and call him five varieties of idiot for not having said
he wanted fried everything. The more he remained
calm, the more enraged I became until Monsieur ended
the problem by pointing out with exquisite logic that
there was one thing we both adored: champagne. He
served it well chilled with my favourite snacks along-
side. Bébé came to sit on my knee for kisses and
Monsieur told me that I should meet Haroun Tazieff,
who was a world authority on volcanoes!

Then the unwelcome and unexpected happened, the
day I finally finished typing the new novel and sent off
the manuscript on time. I'd been in some pain since the
marriage, but had said nothing, because Monsieur was
inclined to stop me working if I felt ill. In the office of
the house where I worked, I put my papers in order,
my pens back in their pot, and then walked out to my
car. The pain had disappeared completely, replaced by
a total lack of feeling on the entire right side of the
body. It took all my strength to lock up the house and
drive the three kilometres back home. On arrival,
unable to park the car because I was suddenly too ill to
do so, I left it in the middle of the square and crawled
up the three steps to Monsieur's door.

My husband took one look at me and called the doctor.
Then he went and parked my car, returning to pack a
small bag of my things to put in his own car, which was
in front of the house. The doctor telephoned a specialist
when he had examined me. Then Monsieur drove me
at Grand Prix speed to the clinic to be 'examined'. The
examination lasted three minutes. Then the surgeon
pointed upwards.

'First floor, madame.'

'Why?'

'You are to be admitted as an emergency.'

Surprise took my breath away and I sat looking at him without understanding his reasons. One minute I'd been finishing my book, the next I was a medical emergency. I was unaware that the lack of feeling and disappearance of pain signalled infection taking hold and spreading. My thoughts were cut short by the arrival of a nurse, who put me into bed and inserted a drip in my arm. Monsieur tried to call my family to inform them of the seriousness of my situation, but they were in Los Angeles and couldn't be located. I was desolate.

Monsieur had told me I'd have to be operated on and I had tried to work out what would happen in an all-French clinic if, after the anaesthetic, I tried to ask for help in English. I lay back thinking black thoughts. We'd been married such a short time and I was in hospital and as ill as I'd ever been. I was unaware that the surgeon had told Monsieur they could not operate in such an infected condition but that they would try to operate in three days' time, when I'd been packed full of antibiotics. In this terrifying period, Monsieur was a tower of strength, sitting, impassive as Buddha, in an armchair next to my bed and anticipating every thought, every need, every moment when I just wanted a hand in mine. He was always there, always loving, always reassuring that of course I would get better.

In the small hours of the next morning my condition worsened and I became so ill I was prepared for immediate surgery. Monsieur told me later that the surgeon had told him, 'It's surgery or the cemetery.' In the operating theatre I was surprised to have a laugh that did me a power of good. In England, theatre staff are severely dressed and masked. Here, I arrived on my metal trolley and was put on the table, naked and chained hand and foot. Shades of the Marquis de Sade!

Then, from somewhere to my right, a very bronzed, handsome young man appeared. He was dressed in emerald with a fuchsia jacket and said softly, 'Shall I put you to sleep?'

'Who're you?' I cried, upset that some tourist had wandered in and seen me gold as a guinea and starkers. By way of a reply he poured something into my drip and I realised my error. I woke some hours later, howling with pain and swearing like a navvy, in French. The young man in the fuchsia jacket returned and administered a magic potion and I slept, watched over by Monsieur. I later learned that this Alain Delon looka-like was the clinic's chief anaesthetist. In France everything is different!

Bébé was sitting on the windowsill waiting, when Monsieur drove me home, at last, from the clinic. I hadn't seen Bébé for almost a month and dreamed of running inside and kissing him to make up for all the weeks he'd been alone again. Instead, I walked slowly, hesitantly, to the house and, feeling my knees wobbling, had to greet him sitting down on the stairs that led to my room before hurrying up to bed. It was only when Monsieur brought my bag in that I realised how much weight *he* had lost. For once in his life my husband had been unable to eat and the tension of waiting so long for me to recover had taken its toll. I told him to lie down on the bed for a minute and the next thing we knew it was five in the afternoon!

Monsieur appeared minutes later with a pot of tea, some biscuits and a jar of honey sent by the husband of my friend Michelle. François has the brainiest bees in Provence and I thoroughly enjoyed every mouthful. Bébé licked the spoon and Monsieur commented, 'When you were in hospital, Bébé ran out to the car twice because he wanted to come and see you.'

'You should have brought him.'

'I was afraid he'd be sick in the car.'

'I'm going to take him to the woods to help me gather pine cones when I'm fit to drive again.'

'He'll break the carrying basket like he did when I took him to see Dr Feat.'

'I shan't put him in the basket. I'll let him sit on his cushion in the front passenger seat and he'll be fine.'

Monsieur swallowed hard, probably wondering if there were police regulations against transporting cats on cushions.

'Now I am married, I shall develop high blood pressure trying to accustom myself to all your ideas,' he said. 'What if he jumps out of the window?'

'Why would he do that?'

'To return to the wild, to be free.'

'If he returns to the wild, he won't have his special chicken dinners and he won't sleep on my bed.'

'You're right, I suppose. He has no reason to want to escape.'

Monsieur went downstairs to the kitchen and made himself a calming pot of lime tea. He was relieved to have his wife home but worried about her condition. It would take months to build up her strength again as she had no appetite. Monsieur sighed. The British didn't understand the joys of food even when they were well, and when they were ill they simply fasted like Indian fakirs. To a food-loving Frenchman the past weeks had been a nightmare. Monsieur decided to ask his wife about dinner. He found her lying back on her frilly pillows, stroking Bébé, who was gazing into her eyes as if hypnotised. He was furious.

'You've just left hospital and you have a cat in your bed. You could catch something terrible.'

'Nonsense! There are far more germs in hospital.'

'What would you like to eat this evening?'

'Some more tea and biscuits.'

'For dinner?'

'It's the best I can do.'

When I finally recovered enough to take Bébé on his first outing, he ran all around the house in sheer excitement. Then he snuggled in my arms as I carried him to the car and installed him in the front passenger seat. We didn't go very far, just out of the village and down the road to the other side of the hill, where I liked gathering fossils, pine cones and other curious objects.

On arrival in the wood, Bébé stood quite still, inhaling the new and fascinating scents of this secret place. Then, having scratched a tree trunk or two, he ran after me, stopping here and there to sniff and leap up at butterflies. For an hour, we played and searched for treasures of the forest. Then, in an eruption of joy, Bébé ran around a nearby field, returning to my side like a faithful little dog, for a kiss and a 'good boy'. I was touched, because it was obvious that he had dreamed of such an outing and the realisation of the dream had made this the very best day of Bébé's life.

Trips to the wood became a regular part of our routine. Once I took Bébé to another forest and the nearby house of friends, but he was afraid of the unknown, walking to heel and barely daring to breathe. It was obvious that his favourite outing was the familiar woodland near the house. From that day on I called it 'our forest' and when I said that Bébé ran to the front door, full of joy at the idea of an hour together, rummaging in the undergrowth or gathering wild fennel at the edge of the field. They were golden moments, never to be forgotten by either of us.

It didn't take long for Bébé to become a writer's cat. He learned the job in about three days. Mornings, Monsieur and I went shopping or to the nearby port of Les Lecques for a coffee. After lunch, in summer, I took an hour's siesta before starting work. I wrote on my bed, as always, and typed at a big table near the window. Bébé assisted by lying on his personal cushion, placed to the right of my hands as I typed, and watching the endlessly moving carriage. His head turned to right, to left, like folk at Wimbledon.

After ten minutes of watching, Bébé slept until six, when it was time for me to join Monsieur for a glass of champagne. First, though, I gave Bébé his dinner. Then, while we drank our champagne, he sat on my husband's knee, purring agreement while Monsieur talked. He was the very happiest cat in the world and soon felt the need to go to his basket to dream of all the surprising things we'd do in the morning. Once Bébé had been the loneliest cat in France, or even in the world. Those days were over and he purred contentedly as he thought how life had changed. I thought how my life had also changed and was content.

Chapter Eight

We had been out to dinner and were home later than usual. I watched as Monsieur parked the car, took out his keys and opened the front door for me. Hearing a faint coughing sound, we put on the exterior light and watched as Bébé ran straight to a small black object huddled near the steps. It was one of the kittens of an abandoned cat, who lived somewhere on the hill, but who came to eat outside our door. The cough was worrying and Monsieur put the kitten in a carton and settled her in the living room, having announced that he would deliver her to the vet in the morning.

Bébé leapt on to my knee to be reassured that he was still the best and most beautiful cat in the world. He was a very clean cat and I knew well that he would keep his distance from the newcomer, in case she had fleas, tics or worse. Despite everything, he was curious and kept gazing at the newcomer, who peeped over the top of her box, a woeful expression on her face. When the clock chimed eleven, Monsieur said he was going to retire in order to be up early to go to the vet in the morning. Bébé and I ran up to my room. He was visibly relieved to be out of danger and, having peered over the balustrade at the kitten one last time, he hurried into the bedroom and leapt on to his pillow.

Dr Feat diagnosed the coryza, a kind of cat flu that can be fatal. Monsieur returned home with a sad face and a large bag of medication.

'She has to have inhalations twice a day. I don't know how I can persuade a kitten who's never been in a house to sit under a towel having inhalations! Vets don't understand how illogical cats can be.'

'Is it a serious illness?'

'Of course it is. If she doesn't have the treatment she could become blocked in the nose and suffocate!'

That afternoon I went out shopping and bought everything Monsieur likes best to eat, planning to make him a giant-sized pizza and a chocolate mousse as black as Grimethorpe Colliery. When I returned to the house, I found Monsieur sitting at table, a towel over his head taking an inhalation. I couldn't resist teasing him.

'I thought it was the kitten who had to inhale?'

At that moment I noticed a black tail projecting from under Monsieur's tweed jacket. Explanations followed five minutes later, when kitten and husband emerged.

'First she scratched me. Then she bit me. Then she tried to jump out of the window. Finally, I prepared the vapour and put her and myself under the towel. Then she began to purr! We shall do it twice a day like the vet said. I must say it's done wonders for my cold.'

Monsieur blew his nose loud and long and then went for a nap on the sofa. A black tail projected from under the tweed jacket, while he and the kitten slept. We named her Pushy, because of her habit of advancing like the Light Brigade when she wanted something. Bébé was so jealous he wouldn't even eat his chicken and the smell of the inhalations made him howl. Life was tense for a while, because Monsieur was the only one who adored the new cat.

A couple of weeks later Pushy was pronounced fit. Monsieur's cold had disappeared and Bébé had day-long sleeps on my bed to compensate for the fact that he had an Everest-climbing cat as companion. In those early days he used to watch from the comfort of the sofa, where he and I had our early-afternoon HQ, while Pushy climbed up the balustrade and then sprang to the picture rail, so she could reach the wrought-iron bars that led to the winter garden and the roof. Bébé was saved from dying of annoyance by Monsieur's affection, double portions of pâté in the evenings and his hours on my bed. In our moments in the forest or eating snacks together, he was as happy as a lark, forgetting Pushy the alpinist and pretending he was Top Cat again.

Around this time the true difference between a French gentleman and an English writer became apparent. In other words, I discovered my husband's passion for mathematics. Knowledge in French schools is Cartesian and a talent for maths a most admired attribute. It makes for a rather dated view of things and Monsieur is not immune. He considers it absolutely essential to make weekly totals of all money spent and on what. This is a habit he learned from his father, who also needed to know how much had been spent on each household category: food, entertaining, clothes, petrol etc. As Monsieur's mama couldn't add up any more than I can, she invented a unique column headed CHARITY, which accounted for holes in the weekly accounts.

I was considering copying this ingenuity, when Monsieur remained stupefied for half a day, after reading that I'd spent a rather large – to tell the truth, enormous – sum on perfume. After this 'overreaction' I opted for falling ill every time the dreaded day arrived for reckoning up chequebook stubs. On seeing what I've spent and on what, Monsieur invariably has to have a strong drink to get over the shock. He tells me that my priorities are not French ones, because food is of little importance. Clothes are bought in English sales and perfume comes from New York. Monsieur considered forbidding all purchases relating to my bedroom, like scented candles, embroidered covers and French linen. Then he decided that he might be undermining the pleasure quotient in his own life if he did that.

Finally, we decided that one of us must sell his or her house to avoid our paying two sets of bills. I therefore put my house up for sale, waited a year and had only one person to view. He staggered out into the street, having climbed all the stairs to the roof terrace. He pronounced the house pretty and old but suitable only for experienced mountaineers! Monsieur boiled with impatience and one day put a card on his entrance door saying FOR SALE. The house was bought four days later by a young couple on honeymoon, who planned to use it for holidays and eventual retirement.

Monsieur loves making lists, and he made them of every item in his home. Then he measured everything that he wished to take with him to the new house. It was mostly furniture that had belonged to his parents, including a Breton cupboard the size of the *Lusitania*, a sideboard resembling the Rock of Gibraltar and some armchairs obviously made for sumo-sized bottoms. He made frequent visits to the other house, trying to accustom himself to the winding stairs, the strangely disparate angles in every room and the fact that it was different. And every evening, on returning home, he took Pushy on his knee to avoid getting bitten, because she didn't care for his long absences from the house.

Bébé glowered at Pushy. What did she think she was doing, sitting on his master's knee at six in the evening, when everyone knew it was *his* time for being spoiled by Monsieur? Bébé was wondering what to do, when he heard Madame drive up outside and ran to greet her. She had been working hard getting the new house ready and had promised him a special place forbidden to Pushy. It would be *their* study and she would write there and he could have his own bed and cushion and a secret niche in which to be snug in cold weather. He could hardly wait to spend his afternoons peacefully with Madame.

At that moment Pushy approached and licked his ears. Bébé loved having his ears licked and purred contentedly. Having had the desired effect, Pushy returned to her master's lap and fell asleep. Bébé watched her out of the corner of his eye, thinking that she was improving now that she was getting to be grown up. Who knows? he thought. Perhaps someday we can be friends.

Knowing how animals hate to leave home, Monsieur had meticulously prepared their removal. Every stool, cushion, dish and bed cover was kept as they had always known them and where they had always found them. Bébé loved the new house at once, because he could watch folk passing in the street from the safety of a specially wide window ledge. Pushy was less enthusiastic, because she had soon realised that Bébé disappeared each afternoon to a room she was not allowed to enter. When this happened, she liked to shin up to the rafters in the double-height garage and glower down at Bébé when he returned and stood, watching her from the floor far below. It was the classic male–female battle and we never knew who won.

Actors such as Boyer, Chevalier, Gabin and Gerard Philippe gave an impression of French sensuality that almost ruined the entente cordiale, because generations of Englishmen became convinced that Frenchmen did it five times a day. The reality is that what turns a Frenchman on is 'steak *frites*', veal stew like his mum made and partridge swimming in Calvados, a liqueur adored by Inspector Maigret. When he overindulges and grows a paunch, the Frenchman invests in a good pair of corsets like my nana's Spirellas. What he never considers is stopping eating.

One day, before leaving for the new house, we were invited to Sunday lunch by the bar owner, who had made our meeting possible. Monsieur warned me that it would last a long time, be in the open air and that I'd best take a parasol.

We were greeted by a dozen guests and the lady of the house, beautiful in a Mexican-style dress. After being introduced to everyone, I was handed a glass of wine and shown the long trestle table where the guests would lunch. There were four glasses by every place and so many knives, forks and spoons that I wondered what on earth was going to be served.

Seeing my apprehension, Monsieur said, 'Today, you can learn to eat like a French person. I can assure you that the food will be perfect.'

'If I eat like a French person, I'll soon weigh two hundred kilos!'

'Do try a little of everything. Otherwise they'll wonder what kind of person I married and if you are displeased with the food.'

The meal started well with eggs mimosa. I love hard-boiled eggs chopped up and scattered on pretty vege-tables and ate all the helping served. Then fresh-cooked sardines were passed round with wedges of lemon. I ate one or two to show willing. A giant foie gras en croute, roast thrushes and a home-cured ham followed for those who were desperately hungry. The sight of the poor little thrushes upset me and I sat looking at my plate and wanting to leave. Wine of every colour flowed like water and the waiters did their best to understand that I drink Vittel. Laughter echoed as new dishes appeared and were served in vast dollops on my plate. Delicious pasta, risottos, stuffed vegetables and ratatouille came and went. A distant clock chimed three, three thirty, four.

I was saved from disgrace by my neighbour at table, a gendarme, who was a legendary eater. When he had finished his plate, he finished mine, smiling delightedly at my reaction to his *gourmandise*. I looked across at Monsieur, who was demolishing a portion of Camem-bert with obvious relish. Then a powerful eau-de-vie was served as a '*trou* Normand' to 'clean the passages', as the gendarme explained, 'in preparation for the sweets'. By this time, my eyes were as wide as saucers, because I'd never seen so much food before, nor such appetites. Panic dawned when the waiter put a giant tarte tatin on my plate covered in a gallon of Chantilly. Out of the corner of my eye I watched the gendarme wolfing down his sweet. Was it possible he could also eat mine? He'd been eating since twelve thirty and had had two portions of everything except the first course. I had no need to worry. When his plate was empty, he took mine and did his human-vacuum-cleaner act!

I drank three cups of coffee to celebrate the end of the meal. The gendarme was still at table when I wandered off to watch the boule players warming up. Looking back, I saw our hostess leaving a pile of chocolates at the gendarme's side, in case the pangs of hunger returned before he finished his coffee.

A game of boules is one of the favourite Sunday occupations in this region. This particular game was unforgettable because of a phenomenon rarely heard in public, a demonstration of epic talent by the senior guest present. Each time he bent forward to take aim with his metal boule, he let loose a mighty fart reminiscent of the guns of Navarone. Fascinated by his timing and sphincter control, I remained hypnotised for a few minutes. No one else seemed to notice, despite the decibels and, fearing that my British sense of humour might not be appreciated, I rushed off to the greenhouse and sat among the passion flowers laughing till I cried at each new echoing boom.

It was some time before I realised that Monsieur was standing outside the greenhouse watching me, his face particularly solemn.

'You should not laugh at such things. In France we are discreet about the intestinal gas of elderly persons.'

'Don't you ever get tempted to laugh?'

'I don't like laughing. I have less than perfect teeth, so I avoid showing them!'

This provoked even greater paroxysms of laughter and, despite his iron self-control, Monsieur saw the joke. Finally, we went to take leave of our hostess and walked slowly home. I told Monsieur how our neighbour, who had been in hospital for two months with a grave intestinal blockage due to concretion, had told me of his terrible sufferings. Monsieur was concerned.

'What did he say?'

'Oh, he didn't talk about the operation or the pain he'd suffered, just his anguish at the food. For three weeks he had nothing but watery soup four times a day. He said it was the very worst thing that ever happened to him.'

Monsieur glanced at me to see if I was kidding.

'I must teach you diplomacy, Hélène.'

'I shall look forward to that and I'll try to teach you spontaneity, but I don't think I'll succeed.'

As the years passed, most of the early differences in our marriage were ironed out. I controlled my incomprehensible British sense of humour and tried hard to eat more slowly. Monsieur tried to hurry up, but without success. Impossible to eat steak and vegetables and fried potatoes together. He eats the steak, then the potatoes, and then finds an excuse to eat the vegetables 'later', in case he doesn't have enough room for the cheese and two helpings of pudding. After that, he retires to his armchair with an indigestion tablet, which he eats because he loves the minty flavour, not because he's eaten too fast.

From the start of the marriage, I did my best to learn French as it should be spoken, but soon realised that to speak the language perfectly you have to have an elasticated mouth, so you can say four vowels at the same time. This caused friends and neighbours to tease me, when I pronounced words wrong. I tried to teach them how English tongues negotiate the 'th' sound, but

the erotic implications of the necessary mouth movements caused the lessons to be abandoned because of
ten-decibel laughter.

The people of this region are unique, perhaps because
of their history. They've survived drought and plague
and the great freeze-ups of the sixteenth century. They
vanquished or absorbed all the invaders, the Greeks,
the Ligurians and probably the Mohicans, the essence
of their character distilled from this dramatic past. They
are a rare breed, with a laconic sense of humour, an
extrovert personality and a capacity for *joie de vivre*
unequalled anywhere in Europe. They love their
children and their customs, and taught me, as time
passed, about the fêtes and processions that are part of
their lives. There are fancy-dress parades for the
children, also for the adults, who once a year put on
costumes resembling the traditional '*santons*', or figur-
ines, of Provence. Monsieur's favourite ceremony is the
thirteen desserts before Christmas, because this gives
him a legitimate excuse to eat thirteen sweets one after
the other.

I gradually became familiar with the characters of the
village. Among them was the archivist and historian,
Monsieur Cachard, who drives a tiny, spluttering car,
wears a beret winter and summer and can trace every
street, arch and studded door back to the twelfth
century. Then there was the village priest, who loved
eating and was fond of a glass of wine. He could also
read between the lines of every situation. Towards the
end of his life I passed him in the street, walking slowly
in his black soutane. When I enquired about his health,
he replied, 'Terrible, madame, but I try to ignore it.' My
fondest memory of the priest was of the first time I ever
saw him, outside a restaurant, eating with friends on

the terrace. They were all laughing, but one sound echoed more joyfully than all the others and I asked a passing villager who had the wonderful infectious laugh. She replied with a knowing smile, 'That, Hélène, is Monsieur le Curé.' If all priests were capable of such *joie de vivre*, the churches would be full.

PART TWO

Cat Chat

'I want so much to give you a real idea of the
simplicity of life here.'
Van Gogh in a letter written in Arles to Theo

Chapter Nine

Our first days in the house were memorable. Pushy spent all her time haring up the stairs to the mezzanine level of the garage. Once she reached the Olympian heights she perched on the narrow balustrade, looking down at Bébé and me as if we were Lilliputians.

Monsieur measured, arranged and rearranged his personal living room, also known as the snug, surprised when his *Titanic*-sized furniture, which had seemed enormous in the other house, now looked normal-sized and perfect in the big ground-floor room.

I tried to find all my files and papers and rushed around like a blue-arsed fly buying bookshelves, architects' lamps and all manner of cabinets to keep the upstairs office-bedroom in some semblance of order. Once my typewriter was set up and the bed, where I write, made up with vast piles of pillows, I felt much better. I did my best to avoid thinking of unpacking and arranging the oversized kitchen/dining room. Instead, Monsieur invited me to the local pizzeria, L'Arlequin.

There, he proceeded to try out each of their specialities. It took some time and made him very happy, because he suffers from serious pizza addiction. He especially loved Eric's pizza with blue cheese and black olives.

Bébé checked out his own priorities: the sofa with his special cushion, the typing table with another personal cushion and the wide window ledges that enabled him to survey the world from ground- or first-floor level. He sniffed his basket for a long time, to make sure the removal man hadn't taken a nap in it. Finally, satisfied, he lay on his cushion and watched the hive of activity all around. Our efforts exhausted him and he woke only briefly to go and make the acquaintance of a near neighbour at the ground-floor window. I'd already heard Bébé 'reply' when the postman talked to him. The young man was delighted and called out to me.

'I never met a talking cat before, madame.'

'Bébé's very gregarious. Have you met Pushy yet?'

'Yes, madame. She bit me yesterday, so I shall only talk to Bébé in future.'

Gradually our routines took their new form, at least their new places, because the routines were the same: breakfast between four thirty and five, outings in the morning, lunch in the village or at home. Then work for me and evenings together discussing everything under the sun, or my being tutored in French crossword puzzles by Monsieur.

In those first weeks we had a few problems in the house, despite all the work that had been done under my supervision. My first shower in one of the new bathrooms was memorable, because, as I stood under the warm jets washing my hair, faecal matter rose from the shower drain and was at ankle level before I noticed. Somehow the pipes to the new bathrooms weren't linked to the correct drains. The plumber informed me he would get it fixed in 24 hours. It took him a week to pierce a small hole in the metre-thick walls and he became irritable and said he preferred working in new houses. I let him go and, having taken the advice of our neighbours, called the local plumber, Monsieur Bernard, whose expertise was vouched for by everyone and who knows all about metre-thick walls. Village rumour has it that, when the mistral blows at force ten, Monsieur Bernard takes off like Concorde, propelled along the narrow streets by his twirly handlebar moustache which is the finest I've ever seen.

We acquired a new family doctor, a handsome gentleman with lazy blue eyes, blond hair and real English tweed clothes. He looks as if he were born in Chipping Sodbury, but his deceptively dreamy personality is pure Scarlet Pimpernel.

This was also the period of establishing links with the village tradesmen. There was the grocer, who immediately realised that I could resist anything except ripe figs, mangoes and local strawberries and that the quantity of Vittel water drunk in our house may well enter *The Guinness Book of Records*. Monsieur Laskri selects lovely cheeses, the best chocolate ice cream and vegetables that taste like vegetables used to. Members of his family work with him and his three-year-old granddaughter, Chloe, already has ambitions to operate the cash register.

Then there was the village butcher, Monsieur Benivady, who is known throughout the region for his sausages, his wife's cooking, his daughter's superb take-away specialities and his own vast knowledge of the lost art of butchery. Monsieur loves his renowned white-wine-flavoured sausages, the sauerkraut, steak tartare and stuffed everything that is on the menu each Friday. A neighbour's dog follows me when I go to the butcher's shop and comes back with a bone. And Bébé waits at the door sniffing in case I arrive with a chicken.

In those early days, I had wonderful times walking for miles trying to 'learn' the streets of the centre of the village of La Cadière d'Azur. Once I passed through the great gates of the most ancient part of the village, I felt as if I were in another world, with winding streets, some with wooden 'bridges' at first-floor level from one house to another. There were stone steps hewn in medieval times that led from the main street via covered tunnels, wide enough for one, to the rue de la Colle. The view from the highest point of the village was of vineyards and the distant mountains of Saint-Baume. In autumn the vines change colour and the fields form stripes of gold, green and russet that turn the landscape into a geometric work of art.

Even the street names hereabouts are fascinating: the rue Tricot des Pères, the rue de Paradis, the rue des Grenadiers and the Montée Saint-Eloi. There used to be a ferocious dog who lived on the Montée, who barred my way every morning when I went for a walk. One day, tired of having to make a detour to avoid being bitten, I made an enormous beef and chicken sandwich before leaving the house. When the ferocious dog appeared to bark and show his biting teeth, I gave him the sandwich and, lying unashamedly, called him a 'good dog'. The next day he was there, wagging his tail and wanting his sandwich. We eventually became friends and years later, after his owner moved house, I was walking high in the village, when a fierce dog barred my way. Then, recognising me, wagged his tail. I had a little cake I'd bought for Monsieur, so I handed it over and said 'good dog'. He ate it with relish, though he would probably have preferred a beef and chicken sandwich.

We had arrived in early autumn, a short but beautiful period in Provence, which has always been my favourite. Once winter came, with its cold nights and bright but icy sun-touched days, we organised the comfort of the house. Each year, the routines are the same: quilts are placed on beds and there's a bed in every room in this house; winter curtains replace the gauzy ones of summer. I bought some canoe-sized lambswool bedroom slippers and despite their hideous appearance wore them all the time in the house.

And Bébé, who, a couple of years after our arrival, began to age fast, had to have a hot-water bottle when he came to watch me type. At night, however, he often had Pushy to keep him warm. Having been the bane of his life in her young days, she had realised that the old gentleman who had once resented her presence now needed her. And so they slept together on my bed, Pushy warming Bébé with her affection, her youth and her soft velour body. At these moments, Bébé purred contentedly and, having looked at me out of the corner of his eye, as I corrected my pages, fell asleep next to his former enemy.

In winter, Monsieur wears his American pioneer shirt, which I bought for him at Bergdorf Goodman, New York, in the early days of our acquaintance. I also bought him a blue cashmere cardigan, which at first Monsieur resisted because 'I am not British'. He then wore his cardy all winter because it was comfortable and once expressed the fear that if the weather turned too cold he might sleep in it. So far he's managed to resist the temptation, but I'm not sure how long he'll hold out. My only bad buy in the States was a pair of Bermudas and matching shirt in burnt orange and coffee Sea Island Cotton. Monsieur resisted wearing the ensemble for years because 'I refuse absolutely to dress like an American'. Then, in one of the hottest spells ever recorded in our region of Provence, he put it on to go to the post office.

'If I dress how I usually do, I shall feel the heat too much. I prefer to be taken for an American. I must say it's a very comfortable outfit.'

The moment Monsieur stepped outside I heard a neighbour call out, 'You look like something out of a fashion magazine, monsieur.' It took him an hour to walk fifty yards to the post office and fifty yards back, because every few steps folk asked him where he bought the outfit and why he didn't dress like that more often. I noted that Monsieur returned, his head held high, risking a quick glance at his reflection in the mirror as he entered the snug. He was visibly surprised by the attention he had received.

'No one thought I was from Miami. In fact they complimented me on the outfit.'

'I'm so glad you feel comfortable in it. You look really great in the colour.'

'Only you could persuade me to wear an orange abstract work of art and like it. And I *love* my new red British cardigan. I'm looking forward to winter because of it. Before I met you I wore navy blue and – '

'More navy blue and, what a surprise, navy blue.'

We laughed together and he held me close, as we both remembered his measuring Bébé's croquettes on a letter scale and wearing closed shoes even in ninety degrees of heat. I'd taught my husband a different angle on life, a taste of liberation from the rigidly established habits of a lifetime. He still resisted just about everything, but not for long. As for Monsieur, he had proved to be the epitome of patience when teaching me diplomacy. Often I became enraged with the lessons that were simple explanations of how French people say things: 'A woman is never old, she's of a certain age,' for instance. He also taught me that women are never fat, even if they have arses like aircraft carriers. I do my best to stop saying it how it is and making Monsieur stagger, but diplomacy will never be my strong point.

My New Year present from Monsieur was an unforgettable surprise. I came home after a few days in London and found a beautiful sofa in my bedroom. I'd admired the sofa and wanted to buy it some months previously, but it wouldn't go through my bedroom door. Looking incredulously at the sofa and then at Monsieur, I asked, 'How did you get it into the room? They said it should not be taken apart and it was much too wide.'

'I called masons and they knocked down part of the wall, passed the sofa inside and then rebuilt the wall. I knew it would make you happy and I so wanted to see the surprise on your face.'

I stared at Monsieur as if he'd sprouted two heads, unable to believe that my seemingly conventional husband had had a wall knocked down and then rebuilt so he could surprise me. I've since learned that once in a while Monsieur has an idea that stops everyone in his tracks. I look forward to these moments of inspiration and often talk about them for weeks. In summer, when it's too hot and heavy to go out, we often sit on the sofa, drinking iced tea and just lounging drowsily in total harmony with each other. And every time I see the sofa I think of that wall and how he had had it knocked down. And I'm happy.

Chapter Ten

Our house has too many stairs, but I love it anyway. Swallows nest under the eaves in springtime and an ancient wisteria from the garden next door climbs up the wall, perfuming the air. The village has been famous for its wine for centuries and the view from the hill is of a patchwork of vineyards as far as the eye can see. Summers here are hot and humid. Walls and distant landscapes oscillate like a mirage in the desert. Winters are predictable, cold and clear, except once in a while when it rains without ceasing. In winter, Monsieur and I hibernate. There are few surprises. At least that is what I used to think.

It was an unusually icy day in April. I was with Monsieur in the snug on the ground floor. We turned up the radiators and kept looking out of the window, wanting to go for a walk, but not liking the idea of being exposed to the skin-stripping wind. Suddenly, a car appeared. The driver stopped outside and threw a heavy object at the glass-paned door. Then he took the bend and disappeared, leaving us staring at what seemed to my short-sighted eyes to be a triangular cat. Monsieur said, 'They've abandoned the cat because she's pregnant.' That explained the triangular shape! I said that under no circumstances should we open the door and feed her. Looking again at the cat, I saw that she was spotless, black and white with a dot over one eye that gave her a lopsided look. She didn't miaow, just stood, wistful and silent at the window, as if wondering what was going to happen to her.

Forgetting all my resolutions not to feed the poor animal, I rushed off to get a bowl of water and some chicken leftovers. I was about to give her the food, when the cat lay down on the stone step of the house, gave a shudder and went into labour.

Monsieur and I observed the usual routines before imminent birth. The outer doors to the street were closed, a basket found and lined, a scratch box provided and a blanket draped over the roof of the basket to keep out draughts. It was five in the evening and, whether we liked the idea or not, we had a new cat. We were both secretly delighted by the idea and in agreement that once the kittens were weaned they could be placed with friends and neighbours.

By ten in the evening, I told Monsieur that the cat, named with great originality Spot, had had three kittens. We placed food and water nearby and left her in peace for the night. Spot was in fine form. We were both exhausted.

I woke at five and went downstairs to the snug, where Monsieur makes our breakfast coffee on a machine only he can dominate. Given my talent for breaking things mechanical, I'm forbidden to touch this hissing, whining relic of times past in case its metal intestines take offence. Monsieur was troubled by the minute size of the kittens. 'They look like little rats,' he said.

I cleaned out Spot's box, changed her water and then peered in to see the kittens. She purred contentedly while I counted: one . . . two . . . three . . . four . . . oh dear me! . . . five . . . six. One was a giant, black and beautiful. The other five were emaciated midgets, one tabby, three black, tan and white and one of a brown mottled ugliness with a blonde spot on the side of her nose. I broke the news to Monsieur that there were six kittens. 'We'll find good homes for them later,' he replied, handing me my morning coffee. And that was that.

To put Monsieur in a good mood, I rushed off to the bakery at the end of the street and bought more croissants. Then I managed to find a couple of words for his crossword puzzle. He was happy and smiling. For the moment, the problem of seven extra cats was temporarily forgotten. When Bébé arrived, however, he looked nonplussed at the new cat. Then, tired and unwell, he returned to his bed in the kitchen. I followed, taking him in my arms and hearing him purr as he always had, when he was confident that I belonged to him and loved him more than any other cat in the world.

For six weeks, Spot was the perfect mother, allowing the Brigade, as we now called them, to suckle day and night, cleaning them, loving them, pushing and shoving them towards some semblance of order. Then she became ill, ran a fever and had to be put in the clinic. She had severe enteritis and would have to remain in care at the clinic to avoid giving it to the kittens.

It was weaning time and I was alone to do what had to be done. I fed them with a product specially formulated for such circumstances. All of them were sick. I made rice water and boiled fish to help their baby digestive systems. By common accord, they all refused to eat such insipid offerings. Then the male, Noir, began to cry for his mother and searched everywhere for his beloved milk pump. The others fell silent and it seemed to Monsieur and me that they were getting thinner by the hour.

Then, one day, friends came to lunch and I made veal blanquette. The Brigade ate more than the guests and Noir also demolished a large part of Monsieur's pear tart with cream. From that moment on it was easy to feed them. The kittens ate with us, consuming prodigious quantities of toast and marmalade, cake, paella, game soup and Monsieur Benivady's home-made raviolis. The tiny bodies put on weight and they began to adventure around my husband's private sitting room, with special affection for his papers, desk and glasses.

When Spot finally returned home, she slept all day long. Deprived of the facilities of the maternal Milk Marketing Board, the Brigade tried mass assaults, but were repulsed with increasing ferocity by their mother. Noir waited till Spot fell asleep and then snuggled up to her to feed. When she woke and sent him packing, we were upset by his pitiful cries. She also began the games that teach young kittens what life is about – imaginary battles with terrifying enemies and her mimicked reactions. Sometimes she got fed up with all of them and went to sleep in an inaccessible place. Then all six cried like babies and sat dejectedly looking around for help.

Dr Feat, our vet, saw the Brigade at this period and told me they had to be wormed. He handed over a long spoutlike contrivance and said I must place it in each kitten's mouth before squirting one measure of worming fluid. I tried it on Noir to begin with, surprised when the others clamoured to be included in this new and novel game. They loved the mixture so much, they followed me around all morning, trying to get second helpings.

At last life was calm again. Then I became ill with an attack of bronchitis and had to have a bed put in the kitchen, so I could supervise the Brigade without climbing up and down stairs. Mother and kittens slept in their basket at one end of the room and I lay in bed at the other. Exhausted by the cough, I positioned myself, as Stanley Holloway used to say, 'in a recumbent posture', watching as Spot continued her lessons in catmanship with her motley crew of ill-balanced offspring. What discipline she meted out, softening only when face to face with the adorable and unique male. For his part, Noir still dreamed of suckling his mother, but Spot remained adamant, which didn't stop him trying every hour of every day.

To begin with, all went well. The kitchen is warm and welcoming. Spot was glad to have a home. The Brigade now had names: Quixote for the brown mottled one, who is the most intelligent of all, Dodu for the plump beautiful one, whose fur is white and tan and black, Pink Nose for the fastest biter in the West, Lunette for the cat whose black-encircled eyes make her look as if she were wearing sunglasses, and Timi for the shyest one of all. I had noticed that, when the Brigade ate, the unassertive Timi was pushed out of the way. It had been the same when they were suckling their mother's milk. Timi had had difficulty getting anything at all. I began to feed her apart from the others, relieved when, at last, she began to put on weight.

Far from trying to be the dominant male, Noir was

obsessed by the desire to return to the days of his baby-hood, when he had suckled hard enough to become the biggest kitten in the whole of France. Exasperated by his persistence and worried by Spot's fatigue, I brought in a second basket, put her in it and left the kittens to the original. The idea was that by separating them I would give Spot the chance to sleep for a few hours each night.

The following evening, I was reading, when Quixote strolled over to my bed. Looking down at the tiny kitten with its comic blonde spot on the nose, I saw challenge in the golden eyes and was relieved that she was too small to climb the steep side of my bed. Seconds later, in a frenetic ascent, claws fully extended into my best patchwork, she arrived. Then she walked to the right and the left, sniffed everything and fell asleep exhausted, her nose next to my neck, where I spray my perfume.

Quixote was followed in the next two days by Pink Nose, Dodu and Lunette. Noir weighed twice as much as the others, so it took him a long time to climb up the bedclothes, with two noisy, unscheduled landings before he finally conquered Everest. He chose my stomach for his pillow and slept immediately, snoring like a child. Surrounded by the Brigade, I looked across the kitchen and saw Timi, the smallest and weakest of the team, watching me over the rim of the basket. Unwilling to exclude one kitten, I went over, put her in my pocket and returned to bed. The Brigade assumed their former positions and Timi chose under my left arm, where she could feel the beat of my heart. She never forgot that moment and has stayed there ever since.

Our routine was established. When night fell, I put

the kittens in their basket and got into bed, coughing like a human Hound of the Baskervilles and sleeping propped up on pillows. Then, one by one, they came, Dodu on my left shoulder, Noir on my stomach, Timi near the heart. When Pink Nose bit her sisters, I exiled her to the floor, so she bit me too. I very nearly bit her back, but decided that kisses and soft words might melt her ferocious heart. It took time, but she became affectionate, attacking only when her brother tried to be bossy. Then, despite the difference in size, she pounced on him and bit him into submission or refuge under the dresser.

Those cold nights in May and early June were memorable, especially when I moved my feet too much. Convinced that there were mice in the bed, the Brigade pounced, bit and burrowed under the clothes to investigate. My big toes acquired battle scars and often I slept in my slippers to avoid complications. The bonus came every morning when Spot and her brood came for their 'hello, my darlings' accompanied by kisses and strokey-strokeys. If an animal's attitudes are formed by its early contacts with human beings, Monsieur and I have produced the only cats in the region who prefer kisses to catfood.

When the kittens were old enough to be given away, no one wanted one. In desperation I asked Dr Feat to help us find good homes for four of them. I couldn't decide which four and was vague on this point. I was saved from decision making by the onset of the tourist season and an invitation to organise three art exhibitions in the local cultural centre. Absent from the house for five hours a day during July and August, I was unaware that callers who rang to enquire about the kittens were told by my husband that there were none left.

September came and the mistral blew hard. One day I asked Monsieur how come all the callers referred by the vet had been informed that no kittens remained. Looking like innocence personified, he replied, 'But Hélène, you were out and I didn't know which kittens were to be given away. You were deliberately vague, because you love them all, as I do.' We finished our coffee, both relieved that the Brigade remained complete. Dodu bit Monsieur's glasses. Noir tried to suckle his mother and received a paw slap. Timi sat in my pocket surveying the scene.

The following morning I commented to Monsieur that the Brigade seemed to be getting fat. Had they had enough exercise during the summer? Monsieur rolled his eyes and put on his logical look. 'I was afraid to send them outside in case they were attacked by dogs without leads. We had so many in summer, to say nothing of the tourists' cars on their way to the hotel garage. I didn't want you to be upset if one of the kittens was injured, so I let them stay in the house.'

'They're six months old and they've never been outside on their own?'

'They can go later.'

'They'll go right now! They're too old to learn from their mother, because she goes chasing around during the day. I shall take them one by one on a lead and teach them the pitfalls of the street.'

Monsieur sat back in his armchair, his face like Patience on a monument. He hated his cats to go out and felt responsible for them 24 hours a day. I believed they should be put out from an early age to become streetwise. It was a subject on which we would never see eye to eye. Nevertheless, I put Quixote on a fine suede lead and off we went walking. I showed her the rain drains where all the cats of the vicinity hid when in danger. We did the entire block twice and then in the following two weeks all the streets and alleys near my house. Quixote walked proud with her tail up in the air, liking best the moment at the end of the walk when we entered the wild garden next door, said hello to the resident feline, Patcat, and played together in the sun.

After two weeks Quixote went out alone and I took Noir on his basic training. Quixote was furious, sure that he had stolen her personal lead, so she marched at my side as she had during her training and then played with her brother in the garden. Noir loved his period of learning and cried buckets when the two weeks were over and his place was taken by Dodu. Like Quixote, he accompanied the new pupil on her walking tour each day and running around the garden next door till he was exhausted and obliged to return to the house for kisses and a lie on the day bed with me.

After three months all the members of the Brigade had learned the street, except Timi, who refused to leave the house. Far from running all over the place, the kittens waited at the door for me and we all went and did our routine training walk together, joined by Frioul, our neighbour Sylvie's tom cat, and Etalon di Trola, the hunting dog from next door, who loves the camaraderie of all this. The only problem we met was folk who told me I should be ashamed of taking cats out on a lead. I said nothing in reply, leaving them to see that very soon the cats were free to go where they pleased, though still they preferred their morning constitutional, even without their leads!

Monsieur worried all the time that the cats would be

difficult to recall to the house. I remembered then that during the months on the bed in the kitchen I had learned that Spot called her kittens by sound. I therefore invented a 'call sign' for each kitten to be sung in my off-key contralto. Probably this was an ordeal for the neighbours but it worked wonders with the Brigade, who each learned the call sign and came running when summoned. The only hitch was that lots of other cats and dogs learned the calls signs and came running, worrying Monsieur that he might end up with fifty cats.

The year of the Brigade's arrival was the year when I grew to love this village. Memories return of the day when three men bowed to me in the post office, and I, stupefied, asked why. 'Because of your husband,' they replied. Further questioning revealed that a letter sent by one of my family to 'the Prince', as a joke, had been taken literally. Explanations followed and we all laughed loud and long when I explained that the 'Prince' title used by the family refers to my late mother's reaction when told of the marriage. 'If Hélène has married again, after all these years, he must be a prince.' Mother always wanted me to marry a prince, but I never did.

It was the year when I found one of my neighbours having what seemed to be a very public orgasm outside the butcher's shop. I watched, fascinated, as she inhaled heavily and panted with longing. When I reached the entrance to the shop she said, 'Isn't it wonderful, Hélène, Sniff, *sniff.*' I could smell only a strong beef-and-onion odour coming from Monsieur Benivady's kitchen. My neighbour said with longing, 'He's making beef daube. I could eat a big plateful right now!' It was nine thirty in the morning, but the French passion for food knows no time limits.

It was the year also when I saw the exquisite beauty of the seasons in the Var. Winter is black branches against a watercolour sky and white blossom pushing through the dark outlines. Spring is a short season of great beauty when the wisteria flowers and the sun shines through clouds of cherry blossom on the hill. In summer the landscape oscillates like a mirage in the heat and the vines are a mass of shiny green leaves and heavy purple grapes. In the early morning, watching sunrise is a spiritual experience and the sea a mass of scintillating flashes.

But my favourite season is autumn, the period of the wine harvest, when men with tractors of ripe grapes rumble along the narrow roads towards the local wine co-operative. Tourists hoot their car horns, trying to make the tractor drivers assume city speeding limits. The drivers know better than to try. They hold out their left arm when turning right and their right arm when going left, just for the hell of it. And the fields of vines turn gold and orange in the mellow sunlight of September.

For Bébé, the winter of life was a daily penance. He now remained all the time in the kitchen, watching me cook or type or work collage. Realising that he could no longer mount the stairs, I'd moved my big work table into the kitchen, so he could sit on his cushion watching, as he always had. He didn't care much for the Brigade, who now lived in Monsieur's quarters. Only Timi came to the kitchen and when she appeared Bébé pushed his plate of dinner towards her, because he could no longer eat. Then he went to his basket and waited for Timi to jump in and lie next to him to warm him. He had tried this with Pushy, but she was now so big Bébé had nearly suffocated. With Timi, he was content and so was she.

One morning, Monsieur told me that Bébé was fading fast. I knew it, but I loved him so much because he'd always been there and he was my special friend, the guardian of our joint happy memories. To keep his strength up, I tried to tempt him to eat, but he was too tired and wanted only to be held close and told he was still the most beautiful cat in the world.

Monsieur took Bébé to the vet. Dr Feat pronounced Bébé's poor condition due to old age and weak kidneys. I began to carry him around like a baby and loved him more each day. When I realised he no longer wanted to eat at all it felt like a personal tragedy. I kept telling myself that the first person in a family who dies prepares a new house for the others so they can be together for eternity. I liked this idea very much, but I liked even more sitting in the afternoon sun with Bébé, listening to him as he purred, as he always had when he was in my arms.

Cats like to disappear to die and Bébé was no exception and one day he went to the garden nearby and hid. I stood at the barred gate watching him, letting him go, moved to tears when he stumbled back and used his last bit of strength to try to leap into my arms. I carried him back to the house and we lay together on the divan in the kitchen. I stroked him gently and kissed the top of his head, where he specially liked being kissed. And I stayed there, never moving, just whispering plans for the future when we'd be together again.

The day Bébé left us, Monsieur sat in silence, remembering all the years he had loved his cat. Pushy stood at the window, waiting for Bébé to come home, increasingly anxious as the days passed and he did not return. She waited at the window for three weeks, just staring out, hoping. She barely ate and couldn't sleep. Then, one day, she realised that he'd gone and wouldn't be back and she came and sat at my side in Bébé's place and looked at me as if I could answer all the questions she needed to ask. Timi clung like glue to me and from that day on slept in my room. As for me, I worked twelve hours a day in order not to dwell on thoughts of Bébé. But in the still of the night I went over every marvellous and unforgettable moment with him. I still do and I always will.

Chapter Eleven

Monsieur couldn't bear the idea of Pushy going out and learning the street like all the others but I felt she must have equal rights and learn to be independent of just about everyone. She ran very willingly at my side while she did her basic training, finishing with a joyous cavalcade around the garden, chased by a large striped tomcat.

My husband was in a state of high tension when we returned, so I tried my best to explain that cats have to be able to get by without their masters, in case we die before them. Monsieur avoids thinking of such hideous possibilities and is confident that, since all his family have lived till their nineties, he will too. His cats will therefore go to paradise before him. No amount of reasoning can make him see that we could have an accident or simply die younger than his ancestors. Monsieur looks out of the window when I try to discuss such things and occasionally I lose my legendary patience and bellow like Taurus the bull.

When I took off Pushy's lead and told her she was a good girl, she reacted by running all over Monsieur's living room and then to the adjacent garage to shin up the rafters, something she hadn't done in months. Then she went to the door and miaowed to go out again. Monsieur was very annoyed.

'Do you realise that I shall now have to live with eight cats who want nothing but to go out for a run in the garden or to get soaked for ten minutes in the rain drain? I shall be ill with worry.'

'Of course you won't. You'll go with them.'

'Hélène, when I go out with them it's very enjoyable, but they won't come back. They only come back when they hear you singing their call sign. And who could possibly sing like you!'

'If you don't cheer up a bit I shall go out again and I'll sing outside your window.'

Monsieur retained his calm, changing the subject to avoid the possibility of having to listen to me sing.

'I gather that Pushy enjoyed her walk.'

'Oh yes, she even stood firm when we met a dog. She hissed at him and then let out a very odd howl.'

'What did the dog do?'

'He ran away.'

'He could have attacked you both.'

'I know.'

'What would you have done?'

'I'd probably have been bitten trying to defend Pushy.'

Monsieur said he had decided that he would have to assist with the cats' outings each morning instead of having his snooze in the armchair. I felt a bit conscience-stricken because his existence had changed so much since the marriage. If he had not met me he would have led life as he always had. Now, often, he was faced with different ideas and unpredictable situations that caught him off balance. I decided to ask him why he had wanted to marry me. Monsieur took the wind out of my sails with his reply.

'I always wanted to meet a Martian, that's why, if you really want to know. It's just that I didn't expect to have Martian cats.'

In the Midi in years long past, drought was the scourge of the region. In summer, village taps dripped with less than a trickle. *Manon des Sources*, the great book by Marcel Pagnol, is entirely based on the envy and theft of a water source. Then, one day, a great canal was constructed and water bills rose, but the desert bloomed. People were happy, because the supply was equal to the demand. Wisteria and arums appeared. Vegetable gardens flourished. It didn't rain often but the water in the canal was abundant, coming, so the locals said, from distant mountains 'where it rains all the time'.

Last winter, I had to ask a local mason to redo the half of the roof, which had not been renewed seven years ago. A daunting price and procedure. The date for the commencement of work was set for the last week of September. It rained. At the end of September it was still raining. The mason finally started on 15 October when it stopped raining. Scaffolding was erected. The old tiles removed. That took three days. Then the heavens opened and it rained again for two and a half weeks. Fortunately the mason had covered the roof with a giant plastic sheet. When the cover blew off in a storm and fell tattered to the ground three floors below, rain entered the roof space and below it my studio. Being a pessimist of distinction, I'd covered pictures and papers with plastic sheeting so apart from the lake to be mopped up there was no permanent damage. The job was finished in appalling conditions at the end of November. When the mason left with his father and brother, we all kissed goodbye as if we'd been through a war together.

In December it rained 24 days out of 31. In January it did the same. Doctors' surgeries filled with folk manifesting every malady from hydrophobia to fallen arches. As all the residents of our region believe that either their brains or their balls will rot if exposed to too much water, their normally expansive way of speaking became subdued and their faces looked more and more like those of Mancunians, who at least laugh at the rain.

In February the sun appeared. In March it got hotter. In April and May we had temperatures usually seen only in August. It didn't rain at all and at the end of May a drought was declared and wine growers talked of going bankrupt – but only talked. In June, I went in my car to Toulon. It rained so hard I could barely see to drive the final two miles. I put the car in the underground car park and hared off to the framer's, entering the shop just before the arrival of cascades of rain the likes of which I'd never seen before anywhere in the world, let alone in Europe. An hour later the streets of Toulon were flooded. I waded back to the car park and drove to the motorway, where normally high-speed drivers were crawling along the slow lane, praying, as I was, that they wouldn't hit a police car, bridge, lorry or, worse still, slide down into the nearby vines. Visibility through fog and downpour was less than five yards.

One morning, I read in the *Sunday Telegraph* that in the years to come Great Britain will have a hot Mediterranean climate and that our normally stoic, poe-faced, stiff-upper-lip population will be replaced by an aria-singing, hysterical and emotive one. The entire Mediterranean coast will become desert and undesirable as a place of residence for anything but camels. I found all this fascinating. Someday I'll have to sell the house and emigrate to the country of my origins in order to continue life in the Mediterranean style.

Monsieur refuses to discuss such a possibility. Educated by priests with medieval minds, he believes that all Englishmen wear bowler hats, even in bed, and that the national dish is lamb covered with mint and vinegar, this being eaten at every meal when we are not eating porridge.

In La Cadière d'Azur the residents are stoic. From the fourteenth century, when the plague arrived in the region, this village has had a rare streak of good luck. Epidemics of everything from the Black Death to the concretion missed La Cadière d'Azur completely, though the Plague took a terrible toll in neighbouring villages. Snow, ice ages, floods and invasions were suffered and survived. Invaders did their best to quell the Cadièrien spirit, but ended up married to local girls. Greek invaders taught the locals how to cultivate the olive with real success, the vines likewise. The silver relic of Saint-André that escaped vandalism and revolution is credited with the fact that the village lived through the worst fate could offer and came through unscathed and even enhanced.

It's probably because of the unusually heavy rainfall in the first months of their lives that all the Brigade like water. One or two want to swim in it and Noir lies in it if he gets too hot in the summer. He is the undisputed leader of the Brigade. When he was small, he ate so much he seemed to be in a perpetual daze and we wondered whether he was subnormal. Then we realised that he's short-sighted. As cats don't wear glasses and can't read vision test cards, we've done all we can to make him aware of dangers and he, in his wisdom, shows us that he's very aware.

One day, during his walk through the long grass, Noir heard a rustle and found himself crossing the path of a *couleuvre*, a big nonpoisonous snake with a disconcerting turn of speed and a nasty bite. Noir broke the cat land-speed record that day, returning home for a long session in the scratch box caused by the shock! No one has yet been able to teach him that a cat can go to the lavatory out of doors. For Noir home is best.

When he was six months old he fell out of the first-floor kitchen window and into the street. Terrified in case he'd been killed, Monsieur and I ran out and found Noir sitting in the middle of the road, looking around in puzzlement. We installed a mesh grille to prevent further leaps into the unknown. This serves as commando training web for the Brigade, each of whom can now rival mountain goats for agility. Noir quickly forgot his fall, because it was teatime. Most days, he shares Monsieur's cake or tart and would like to try a saucer of tea, but my husband says cats don't drink tea. Noir makes do with an occasional champagne spillage, though, that makes him snore.

Dodu is beautiful. She's also a talented football player, pickpocket and seductress. She loves ambushing the buttons on Monsieur's shirts, stealing his glasses and using what little aggression she possesses on my typewriter. On hearing the machine, Dodu springs to the table, rises on her hind legs and boxes the 'golf ball' as it moves back and forth. Then, exhausted, she sleeps, with her paws in the air, one eye half open in case she misses something.

Dodu detests the dustbin men's lorry and tourists who shout 'Oh, what a lovely cat' when she's taking her siesta. She's happier since we installed a second wire mesh at the window of the ground floor, after a passer-by lifted up his two dogs 'to play with your cats'. As one of the dogs was a Doberman, Dodu was unconvinced that play was what he had in mind.

Lunette is a champion purrer and snorer of the group, producing a high trilling sound when she's on Monsieur's knee. As he's no mean snorer in his own right, they make a musical partnership when feeling drowsy. At night, Lunette sleeps on a wicker chair covered in one of Monsieur's old tweed jackets. In the middle of the night, if I go down to the kitchen to make tea, find a bottle of water or eat an overlarge sandwich, Lunette comes with me to have a little snack. She rarely needs to be corrected, except when she does her flying-cat imitation on the dresser. If admonished, she tilts her head to one side, listens and then goes to hide under Monsieur's bed.

Pink Nose is almost all white, apart from her black and tan spots. She has pale-green eyes and runs the gamut of feline emotions, provoking reactions from 'darling cat' to 'horrible little monster' every half hour. If a cat can have a sense of humour, Pink Nose has one. She once traumatised Monsieur for three days by munching his stereo speakers. He erected barriers to stop her. She circumnavigated all of them. He rearranged the furniture and hid the speakers. Pink Nose found them. I finally told him to stop leaping up and shouting in desperation every time Pink Nose sprang on the speaker.

Missing the amusing sight of a distraught man rushing back and forth in the living room, Pink Nose transferred her energy to tearing the cover from the underside of Monsieur's bed. He had learned his lesson and pretended to be calm. Rosy puce with stress, he sat tight till Pink Nose went to the window and began clacking her teeth at the pigeons on the roof of the house opposite, forgetting him completely.

Once ugly, Quixote is now considered to be one of the most beautiful of our cats. Her fur, formerly dull brown, has developed into what the French call 'écaille de tortue', tortoiseshell, brown with blonde and auburn highlights. Her eyes are vivid golden yellow. Quixote likes running in the adjacent garden and being invisible. No one can find her when she does not wish to be found. Lucid, stable, affectionate, Quixote is Timi's best friend. She has taught Timi how to avoid the tourists who drive at high speed up the narrow streets, rarely seeing children, cats, steps and drainage channels. She and Timi go to the vet's together and play together. Timi does not share Quixote's talent for chasing tom cats, but no doubt she'll be a late developer. After all, she was three before she agreed to go outside the house. Now she's catching up fast.

Timi is my cat. She sleeps in my room and shares my work table. She is more jealous than any husband, though she wouldn't dream of admitting it. Patience is Timi's virtue and silence her offering, at least during working hours. During the day, she lets her brothers and sisters approach me, simply watching out of the corner of her eye to test my resilience to Dodu's charm. But in the evening and at night no one is allowed in my bedroom, which Timi views as her own special territory. She has a much-loved routine. Eat dinner alone, served by me on her own plate. Then look through the window for a while because birds mass in the evening and Timi is very fond of eyeing their manoeuvres. Then we play, rolling bits of wastepaper into balls for Timi to catch and she becomes by turns a helicopter, a world-class high jumper and a cunning little fox. Finally, exhausted, she gets up on my bed and lies at my side while I scratch her jowls. Then she snores softly till four in the morning, when we get up and go downstairs to say good morning to Monsieur. For the moment, Timi pretends to ignore the amorous advances of Frioul, the tom cat next door. Her world is the studio and my bedroom. Someday, she'll grow up and all that will change. Until then, she seems set to be the only cat ever to exhibit her pictures in collage.

Timi's greatest talent, however, is making herself invisible. I think she learned this from being a baby, in order to avoid battles with her more aggressive sisters. Often, when I want her to go downstairs to eat in the garage and be sociable with Monsieur and her sisters and brother, Timi disappears. I have often searched every room and not found her. When I enter my bedroom, however, I always find Timi walking to heel. Where she came from, where she hides, no one knows. Houdini was surely one of her ancestors.

Chapter Twelve

Winter passed without problem. The Brigade slept most of the time in their baskets or on the day bed in Monsieur's quarters. In this house, our having a bed in every room is not due to excessive eroticism on our part, but to my back, injured seriously twice in twenty years, which makes sitting down much less comfortable than lying down!

In Provence, spring comes in February with the almond blossom and the incessant drone of cement mixers. Everyone starts work on his house, repairing damage from rain or the legendary mistral wind. The beautiful girl who lives opposite can be seen climbing on the perilous heights of her second-floor balcony, treating the wood in readiness for the drying effects of the sun. One of our neighbours observed that his priceless collection of antique motorbikes might be in danger of covetous hands if he didn't burglarproof his cellar. He proceeded with lots of panache and frequent renderings of arias from *Rigoletto* to produce a metal screen that is a work of art and that, at the same time, hides his collection from prying eyes. Beautiful Sylvie gets out her wind-surfing board and takes her daughters to the sea. When she's not being a water nymph she uses a Black & Decker on the interior walls prior to decorating the entire house, fortunately small.

I've always treated the wood at the exterior of the terrace and ground floor, but apart from that have never painted anything myself. Now, inspecting the house, I saw that something had to be done. I wrote off for estimates for painting all exterior woodwork, didn't get a single reply and so phoned around and said I'd call back in a few days to have a price. In the meantime, I applied wood conditioner to the front door and then to the terrace paintwork. The morning after I finished this tiny job, I received the first two telephoned estimates, which made me stagger as if I'd been shot. The third and only other estimate was half as much again as the first two. Monsieur asked politely what was wrong.

'You've gone a bit pale. Shall I make coffee?'

'I had the estimates this morning. They want ten thousand francs for the garage doors and two sets of shutters and ten thousand francs per room for painting the inner rooms. It's ten years since the walls were painted. We'll have to do something.'

Monsieur's eyebrows shot up and he looked at me, his face serious.

'In my youth it cost ten thousand francs for the whole house and that was old francs! We shall have the paintwork washed and hope it can last a few more years.'

'It won't. It's in an awful condition. No, I shall paint the garage doors at least, because they won't wait any longer.'

Monsieur looked at me out of the corner of his eyes

and, knowing that I had no experience at all of painting anything but pictures, said 'Buy a *very* tiny pot of paint.'

Once in a while nationality differences surface in our marriage and this was one of them. I replied that I would do the garage doors and the whole house exterior woodwork with the exception of the attic. Ever wise, Monsieur sat like Buddha in his rocking chair and read the local paper. 'Buy just a *tiny* pot of paint,' he repeated.

I bought three huge pots of dark-green paint and did the garage doors and the ground-floor shutters. My bad back prevents me lifting heavy objects, so I had to do the shutters *in situ*, which meant being a contortionist with gorilla-length arms. The Brigade had to be banished because of a communal desire to assist me and Lunette's avid curiosity about the taste of green paint. The weather turned suddenly hot and I sweated so much I looked like an elderly Silvana Mangano, wet through in the rice fields.

It took a month. My back was so painful that I was impossible to live with. Monsieur resolved the frequent dramas by ordering large quantities of champagne, to be drunk after the day's work. This speeded me up no end and, when the exterior was finished, the cost of materials, champagne and my free if inexpert services cost one-tenth of the local man's estimate.

Delighted to have made an economy for once in my life, I went on a serious painting jag. I did the kitchen/dining room, one of the largest rooms in the house. Then I spent four days in bed, poleaxed by pain. Timi loves it when we are 'ill', because, when I stay in bed, she comes with me, climbs on to her cushion and sleeps all day. Unfortunately, she doesn't sleep all night and wakes at two in the morning wanting breakfast. I was soon better, however, aided by my favourite medication.

Bollinger's profits rose to an all-time record and my appreciation for their produce likewise. After the kitchen, I did the entrance hall, stairs and studio. By then, Monsieur was too exhausted watching for me to continue.

On 1 July, I opened my summer studio to the public. Noir loved the weeks of summer, when the door of Monsieur's ground floor was wide open all afternoon. Sometimes he sat with me on the adjacent steps. Sometimes he hid behind Sylvie's giant plant pots. Often he came inside for kisses and croquettes.

The first time Noir met strangers in the room where I showed my work, he dived under the Breton cupboard and pretended he wasn't there, emerging after their departure and searching the room to make sure they were really gone. Some visitors came with big, unleashed dogs, which is against the law in France. Noir wisely stayed under the cupboard, his instincts for self-preservation always well to the fore.

Then, one August afternoon, the biggest dog of all appeared. At that moment, for reasons unknown, Noir came out, hunched his back in order to seem enormous and then made a sound like a Comanche war cry. The dog fled, was almost hit by an oncoming tourist's car and then set upon by Etalon. The owner complained that my cat had terrified his dog. I didn't bother to reply. After all, a small black cat versus a Great Dane is hardly equal combat. Instead, Noir and I went outside and sat on the steps with our friend Etalon, my walking companion whenever I notice my four stomachs in the mirror and decide I must do something about them.

Noir's greatest summer treat was helping Annie, wife of Etalon's master, when she came each afternoon to throw buckets of cooling water into the rain drains. He discovered that water runs fast downhill and chased it to the bottom of the street and then ran back again. This unaccustomed high level of exercise made him eat like a horse before falling asleep and snoring loudly at six thirty every evening.

As summer reached its height, Noir was joined in his water games by Frioul, the tom cat who lives opposite, and Dodu, Pink Nose and Quixote, who all fancy swimming the Channel. The consumption of cat croquettes increased fivefold and a great time was had by all. All too soon the chill winds of autumn came in September and the leaves began to fall from the plane trees. Once the studio closed, I looked back on my summer visitors and those who, for some reason, had been especially memorable: the beautiful Parisian student, who said honestly that she had no money for a picture; the English couple of natural elegance, who bought a 'tweed' in collage.

A man who asked questions was particularly remembered for all the wrong reasons. He said to Monsieur that anyone who had nine cats should see a psychiatrist, because no 'normal' person could cope with the odours. Monsieur assumed a Louis XIV silence. I, who have been trying so hard to learn some semblance of diplomacy from my husband, failed in this case and heard myself reply, 'If I can cope with the odours of sweaty tourists who come to see the pictures, you can be sure I can survive nine cats.'

The tactless gentleman left without a word. I looked across at Monsieur, wondering what he was going to say about this appalling lack of politeness. He had a faint smile on his face as he spoke.

'We'll go out to dinner to that new restaurant in the village where they do Provençal specialities.'

'I had a little lapse in my lessons of diplomacy. I thought you might be annoyed.'

'If there is one thing I've learned from you, Hélène, it's that there's a time for diplomacy and a time for one of your "knock out the enemy" phrases!'

At four thirty on a late summer morning, I give visiting cat regulars their breakfast and then, when Monsieur has made coffee, the day begins. Dawn is spectacular in summer: at first pale viridian green, then yellow turning to rose. It's the time of day when I'm at peace with the world, before phones start ringing to spoil everything.

I was sitting on the ancient stone steps of the neighbouring house, having a second cup, when I saw what looked to me to be the biggest rat in Provence. Three cats were watching him with interest as he entered the rain-drain tunnel. They didn't give chase, their expression seeming to be one of intense curiosity. I rushed inside and told Monsieur.

'I've just seen the biggest rat in the whole region. Even Spot and Noir were stupefied.'

'Did they run after him?'

'No, they just sat looking on as he went into the rain drain.'

'Then it wasn't a rat.'

An hour later, I heard the plate of croquettes rattling in the space between our inner and outer doors. Monsieur heard it too and went to investigate. Cats eat without making a noise. They don't rattle plates and make themselves conspicuous. I thought of the giant rat and wondered if he had a fondness for cat croquettes.

Then Monsieur returned and, having poured himself another cup of coffee, explained the origin of the noise.

'Your biggest rat ever was a hedgehog. He's eaten the plate of croquettes.'

The following morning the hedgehog returned, ate all the croquettes and ambled off, watched by the entire Brigade. We christened him Harold Rat Hedgehog and quite looked forward to hearing him rattling his plate at five in the morning. Then, one day, he didn't arrive. I looked around the silent streets, afraid that he'd been flattened by a speeding car. The cats also waited for their strange new friend to appear, but Harold Rat Hedgehog stayed away.

Three days later, as dawn was breaking, Harold reappeared, ate as if he were ravenous and ambled off as usual. Reassured by his light and jaunty stride, Monsieur and I were as happy as five-year-olds. A short time passed and then Harold Rat Hedgehog reappeared, followed by two baby hedgehogs. Realising our error, we rechristened her Hilda Rat Hedgehog and marvelled at the beauty of the babies, who followed their mother to the garden next door when she had finished crunching her croquettes. The cats never attacked. Sometimes they followed Hilda Rat Hedgehog and family to see where they were going. When the cats ventured too close, the hedgehogs formed prickly balls, but not for long.

We never did discover where Hilda Rat Hedgehog lived, because she and the babies put on an unaccustomed turn of speed once they reached the long grass. Even Patcat, the ferocious boss of the garden, couldn't find them. The hedgehogs visited until the chill of autumn arrived. Sometimes Hilda Rat Hedgehog and the little ones sat in the corner of the doorway watching as the Brigade chased one another in the half light of dawn. When the sun rose, they disappeared, because they knew that human passers-by, motorists and dogs would not be as welcoming as the residents of the House of Cats.

Chapter Thirteen

The Brigade adore the car, at least when it's in the garage. They sleep on lamb's-fur rugs on the roof, if not in their personal baskets. From the beginning, I wanted them to be used to car travel, but Monsieur always vetoed the idea, on the grounds that it was surely illegal. And so time passed and the Brigade remained home birds.

Then Quixote began to take short rides with me. Noir wanted to but his in-built caution made him afraid. Once, he entered and I drove him slowly up and down the street. At first the movement frightened him. Then he discovered the piles of pillows and cushions in the rear and, by the time we returned to the garage, he was sleeping peacefully.

Still I was worried that they had never learned what should be learned. I work on the Boy Scout principle of 'be prepared' and feel I should be ready to take the Brigade anywhere in an emergency. I made this the excuse for a trip to the beach in the early dawn hours.

I planned to have a run along the beach with them, then come home for breakfast. Monsieur said no on the grounds that I wouldn't get beyond the end of the street and, if I did, the gendarmes would intervene. I had a few doubts too, but mainly on account of Timi's nerves and Lunette's bladder.

Finally, I put Timi and Quixote in one cat carrier and Noir in the other, and the rest lay like odalisques by Delacroix on the cushions. I drove at a stately pace, thinking that, as the French sleep late on Sunday, we were unlikely to meet much traffic. The Brigade remained silent, apart from Noir, who from time to time, when I drove over forty kilometres per hour, let out his Comanche war cry.

On arrival at the beach road, I opened the rear door and gave the familiar order, *'Allons y La Brigade'* – in other words, 'Let's go!' No one moved. Noir was gazing intently at the sea fifty yards away, his ears pricked to the sound of the waves breaking on the rocks. The girls don't move until Noir does and just sat staring unhappily in my direction. I walked to the sand. No one followed. I played with pebbles, hoping the noise would attract them. Nothing happened, except that Noir fell asleep and one or two of his sisters followed suit. After ten futile minutes, I drove off, in the direction of my favourite café, where, having left the Brigade in the car, I ordered a pot of tea and a few fattening brioches.

I was reading the local paper and waiting for my tea, when I realised that Timi was sitting on the chair next to mine and Noir was nearby, licking the croissants on the serving dish. I'd left the driver's-side window open! Panic-stricken, I rushed across the road, opened the car, closed the window. It was too late. There were no cats inside. I ran and searched the nearby stretch of beach.

Nothing. Returning to the café, I heard the owner say, 'They all love my croissants, Hélène.' And there they were, sitting contentedly on the formica tables, licking croissants. I drank my tea, ate a brioche and watched as Dodu charmed the owner's wife.

Having paid the bill – one tea, one brioche and eleven croissants – I called the command, '*Allons y La Brigade*!' and this time everyone followed me, joyful at our marvellous adventure. The sea had been an unknown quantity but Noir and Quixote knew about cafés, because they'd arrived uninvited once or twice in La Cadière d'Azur, having followed me from the house. I drove home slowly, wondering how to tell Monsieur what had happened.

He was outside the house, watching for the car. He'd already opened the garage doors and I reversed in and let the cats out. Monsieur spoke with a twinkle in his eyes.

'How did they like the sea?'

'When they heard it, they wouldn't leave the car.'

'And after?'

'They came in the café and licked eleven croissants!'

Monsieur made coffee and recounted how Jacques, his friend, the fisherman from Bandol, had telephoned.

'He couldn't wait to tell me the news, because he'd never seen six cats in a café before. He said you'd cried, "*Allons y La Brigade*", and they all ran to get back in the car. They'll end up famous, you'll see.'

Since their adventure, the Brigade have kept to their usual territory, their beloved garden adjacent and the streets around the house. But every time I open the back of the car they all leap in and make themselves comfortable on the cushions. I haven't repeated the experience, though perhaps someday I will.

One morning, Monsieur told me I had '*le fluide*' where animals are concerned. I looked this up in the dictionary and found that it means I have a mysterious something that makes animals trust and follow me. When I go for a walk, I often end up with three dogs, two cats and anything else on four legs that feels like a jaunt. Monsieur was giving me warning that we had enough cats. I think he'd overlooked the fact that *he* had wanted to keep all the Brigade and that if he were suddenly a millionaire the first thing he'd do would be to buy a house with a garden in which he could construct a cat recreation centre, to give him the excuse to have 75 cats or even a hundred. Anyway, I nodded obediently and said I wouldn't dream of taking in another cat and he mustn't either. Monsieur always says the same thing when I say that.

'But Hélène, I didn't take in all these cats. You did.'

I don't argue, no point. Monsieur is as stubborn as Murphy's Mule about such things, so I take the blame for the large cat population of the house, which suits me fine.

My birthday falls at the end of August and in the afternoon I sat on the outdoor steps, drinking a celebratory glass of champagne and tickling Noir's stomach. Dodu was perched on my knee, licking the sweat off my arm. Pink Nose was nearby, staring fixedly into space. Following her regard, I saw a cat watching us from the curved staircase of a nearby house. I'd seen the same cat for two or three days, always on the stairs, as if waiting for someone. I was unsure if I'd seen her in the area and couldn't understand what she was doing sitting on the steps, night and day for three days, of a house whose owner was on holiday.

Looking at her, I admired the subtle beige graded to chocolate brown of her ears and the opulent off-white and milky coffee of her body markings. As my eyes caught hers, she stared intently at me. It was a hypnotic gaze that only Siamese with their slightly crossed eyes can accomplish. Then, remembering Monsieur's lecture on my extraterrestrial fluid, I hurried inside.

We were discussing what to have for dinner, when the Siamese ran in, ate a plate of croquettes and ran out again. Monsieur opened his mouth, closed it and then looked hard at me.

'Have you talked to that cat, Hélène?'

'Not a word.'

'Have you stroked her?'

'Never!'

'Well, it's too hot to close the door and I don't suppose she'll come back.'

The clocks struck five. Monsieur poured me another glass. Suddenly he started as the Siamese returned and leapt on the day bed where I was lying, crawled on to my chest and fell asleep, as if she'd arrived at the winning post after a long, hard race. I closed my eyes to avoid Monsieur's gaze, but he got up and came and peered down at the cat.

'She's very beautiful, but who is she?' he asked.

'I've no idea.'

'I shall put her out when she wakes.'

'Of course you will.'

'I don't know what to do about your fluid. The English are a very odd race. They don't like eating, probably don't have time. They spend all their time bewitching animals!'

'You like animals too,' I reminded him.

'I do not provoke every animal in the region to follow

me! Thank goodness we don't live in the jungle. I should have to eat with anacondas and sleep with sugar grubs.'

Exhausted by his exasperation, Monsieur dozed. I secretly christened the Siamese Belle. Looking down, I saw she was watching me. Her eyes were dark blue and her face had something in it of a rabbit, which I found endearing. But it was time to make Monsieur's dinner. I put Belle on the doorstep and ran upstairs to the kitchen.

After dinner, Monsieur was in a very good mood, because I'd made three desserts and he'd eaten all of them.

'She was a very beautiful cat, that Siamese,' he said. 'I'm sorry you had to put her out.'

'Me too.'

Monsieur went to the window and looked towards the staircase, where Belle had spent the last three days and nights.

'She's not there. Where can she have gone? Do you think her owner returned and took her away?'

After coffee, Monsieur announced that he was going to the snug to watch the Grand Prix transmission. He loves watching sport on television, sweating profusely as he drives every inch of the way with his favourite champions and entering a state of exhaustion by the end of the three weeks of the Tour de France cycle race.

I was putting the dishes in the washer, when I was astonished to see Belle looking at me from behind a pile of typing paper. I knew I must put her out of the house. Instead, I showered her with kisses, gave her her dinner, put a bowl of water, cushion and other necessities within reach and left her to sleep. I forgot to tell Monsieur that my 'fluid' was working overtime and went upstairs to the studio, so as not to disturb his enjoyment of the Grand Prix cacophony.

The following morning, I went downstairs for my early-morning coffee with Monsieur and found him with Belle on his knee. He was smiling happily, which I found reassuring.

'I found her in the kitchen when I went upstairs to get coffee from the store cupboard.'

All went well till the Brigade arrived and started sniffing the newcomer. Belle kept quiet throughout the inspection and then took off to have a good look around the garage, situated next to Monsieur's snug. When she returned, Pink Nose was on Monsieur's knee. Every morning she has her spoiling session and adores it. Monsieur was listening intently to the French naval weather forecast, in case he decided to take a cruise in a submarine, when the gentle calm of early morning was shattered by a terrifying cry from Belle in full charge. She had seen Pink Nose on *her* person's knee. The legendary 'territorial fixation' of the Siamese had made itself known. Monsieur's knees were *hers*. Her scratch box was *hers* and no one else could use it. Her sleeping quarters were *hers* too. Belle pinned Pink Nose in the corner with every intention of killing her. We managed to separate them and I rushed upstairs with Belle, returning her to the kitchen, which became her home.

Over many weeks we tried hard to integrate the cats, without success. Belle was impossible, Attila the Hun with the Brigade and utterly adorable with Monsieur and me. Segregation seemed the only answer and that's how it's stayed. Belle gets on well with Spot, for whom she appears to have an enormous admiration. When it's hot, they sit on the neighbour's window ledge and

Monsieur and I sit in front of them, getting our bottoms cooled on the stone bench. Belle's respect for Spot is of unknown origin. Did Spot help her when she was abandoned? We'll never know, but we know that she never growls, bites or starts running amok when Spot is at her side.

It was almost a year before we learned Belle's story. She had belonged to an old lady who lived in the next street and who adored her and spoiled her to death. When the old lady died, Belle remained some days in the cemetery sitting on the grave, before returning to what had always been her home. Two nephews, who had arrived to sort through the papers of the deceased, put Belle outside. At some point afterwards, she gave birth to a kitten, whom she loved. Someone drowned the kitten.

It was only on hearing her story and learning where she had lived that I realised I had met Belle once before, sitting alone outside the house that had been her home. She'd looked so forlorn I'd given her some ham from my shopping bag. Had she remembered that? After all her sad adventures had she found the person who had given her something to eat? No one will ever know. One thing is certain: it took a year to stop her panicking in the face of a closed door. Now, she has learned that at night the doors are closed, but in the morning, at dawn, they open again.

Her passion for one of my leather gloves was harder to fathom, until we learned about the lost baby. I put the glove in her basket and she sleeps with it. Someday, when she's fully recovered from all her traumas, she won't need it any more.

In the meantime, Belle's a remarkable cat and affectionate to a fault. I still cherish the memory of the day when she chased a dog down the street because he pee-peed against *her* wall. She won't let anyone come into the kitchen unless she's quite sure they love cats and can tell an 'enemy' at twenty paces. Her favourite visi-tors are two Parisians, who also have a Siamese. Françoise and Michel are greeted like royalty and Belle has to be discouraged from taking her place at table to eat with everyone!

Monsieur was sure he would have difficulty getting used to Belle. Instead, in a week, they'd formed an after-lunch siesta partnership that has to be seen to be believed. It has the appearance of an ancient Japanese ritual. Monsieur gets on the day bed in the kitchen, arranges his pillows and opens his book. Belle springs up and lies on his legs with her back to him. Monsieur reads. As usual, his after-lunch literary aspirations last five minutes at most. Then he lets the book fall and snores lightly. Belle turns, crawls to his shoulder and sleeps like a log for an hour. Then they go outside for their rendezvous with Spot, unless the wind is strong, in which case the siesta gets extended to three o'clock.

I knew Monsieur had really accepted Belle the day when a passing visitor stopped outside the house, looked at her and then turned to my husband.

'That cat squints.'

Monsieur stood tall and replied with dignity. 'I hadn't noticed.'

'You hadn't noticed? Horrible-looking animal. What is it exactly?'

At this point, Monsieur picked Belle up and turned towards the house.

'This, monsieur, is a very rare animal, part Siamese, part rabbit. Good day to you, monsieur.'

With that, he left the visitor open-mouthed and turned

his energies to making coffee. We laughed, because Monsieur had repeated my joke that Belle's mother was pleasured by a rabbit. Outside, the visitor continued on his way. We heard him saying to his friend as they passed the open window, 'We didn't have things like that in my youth. Never heard of such a thing – a cat crossed with a rabbit. Disgusting!'

Chapter Fourteen

The autumn wine fête was memorable. Huge carthorses of great beauty drew a wagon full of barrels of red wine into the village square. Men decorated every surface of the square with grapes, vine leaves and ancient wine-making implements. Villagers by the dozen mixed with tourists by the hundred and there were demonstrations by the local folk-dancing troupe and their flute and pipe minstrels. Trestle tables were set up in front of the town hall with food of all varieties and more wine to be served.

Everything was beautiful, the village lit by golden sunlight that formed lacy patterns as it filtered through the green leaves of the plane trees. The sky was deep blue, the pavements pale and dusty. Wasps buzzed around the barrels and stung one lady in an unmentionable area, which she reported to the town hall. The Mayor didn't offer to suck out the sting, though no doubt the lady would have found it amusing. And everywhere hazy-faced tourists wandered the narrow streets of the old town searching for the car park – *which* car park, as usual, they couldn't recall.

The villagers of La Cadière d'Azur love the wine-harvest period and the heady smell of crushed grapes that floats in the air during the last weeks of September. That afternoon, I heard one of my neighbours singing a selection of his favourite pieces from Italian opera. Another, well known for his capacities with the 'ladies' of Toulon in the distant days of his youth, fell asleep on a shaded bench, leaning at an angle of 45 degrees, to the intense astonishment of passers-by. In his summer straw hat and his faded beige trousers he cut a fashionable figure, defying the pull of gravity and sleeping as if suspended from an invisible wire. One or two visitors photographed him as a souvenir of their splendid afternoon and a lady from the old people's club commented that Gaston was as famous as any local monument, at least for the day.

After the wine festival, the ladies of the Old People's Club, known as L'Age Tresen, began their distillation of the vin d'orange in preparation for the Christmas sale. At this much-loved event, Cadièriens of all ages visit the premises and buy handmade and home-made gifts for friends and family. Everything for babies is crocheted or hand-knitted and there are pretty cushions, aprons, scented pillows and silk scarves with meticulous neat hems. Hand-knitted gloves, socks and inner socks are a boon in winter and the selection of jams has already put kilos on my numerous bottoms and stomachs. My favourite purchase last year was three pairs of inner socks, one orange, one red and one mulberry-coloured. I wear them all the time in the house and will soon have spreading feet to match all my other spreading regions.

Sometimes, the ladies of the club talk of the village as it was forty years ago when there were four grocery stores, three butcher's shops and the local brothel, the Casa del Sol, where Monsieur Gaston was a champagne-drinking regular, eager to try out all the new arrivals. In those far-off days olive growing and viticulture were the principal occupations with a few stonemasons to keep things in order. The old ladies remember, but few regret the distant past. They are better cared for now and life is calm. The plane trees still line the square and most of them know they will live until they're a hundred.

Belle had been with us for three months when one morning I found her strangely listless. When I picked her up and kissed her, she showed signs of pain in her rear end. Investigation showed an angry red and violet area that had not been there the previous day. I put Belle into her own personal carrying basket and drove her to see the vet.

Belle did a quick tour of Dr Feat's office and stood nice and still while he examined her and took her temperature. The verdict was that she had an abscess next to the anus and would have to be operated on. I looked uncertainly at Belle, who was gazing in cross-eyed admiration at Dr Feat, and left her there. Since her arrival in our home she had never been separated from us and had surely never been to see a vet before. I wondered how it would affect her and how Monsieur and I were going to manage to avoid developing an anxiety neurosis by the end of the day.

All through the morning, lunchtime and afternoon. Monsieur and I looked at our watches, impatient for the evening when I'd bring her home. As we knew nothing of Belle, neither her age nor health nor previous illnesses, we were apprehensive and it was a great relief to get in the car and rush off to Dr Feat's surgery. There, I found a bewildered Belle, still groggy from her anaesthetic and sporting a wide plastic collar, like a loud hailer, fixed around her neck to stop her attacking the stitches in her rear. 'It must stay in place for a week,' the vet said. Belle got into her basket and sat in utter misery watching me.

Once back in her kitchen, she began to try to take off the plastic collar. I took it off for her so she could eat and then put it on again, distracting her from thinking about the collar by lying down and taking her in my arms, her head supported on my shoulder. She loved this and purred at last and then, suddenly, fell asleep. I got up, fixed a special box for her with a big firm pillow underneath her and another for her to rest her head. The next week would be spent dosing Belle with all her medication, taking off and putting back on the hated plastic collar and trying to cajole her into a good mood by working all day and every day at my table in the kitchen doing collage. Belle loves it when I do collage and she lay, her head on the support pillow, watching happily until she fell asleep. When I didn't work I took her in my arms and lay with her on the day bed, and that she liked even more.

The outcome of all this spoiling was that Belle howled her protests when she was well again and no longer had me around all day and every day. I've always thought that children and animals should have constant attention when ill. Belle made me doubt the wisdom of this, at least in the case of cross-eyed Siamese-rabbit cats. It was Monsieur who solved the problem by offering to lie on the day bed with Belle for a 'little longer' than usual.

Their siestas now last till mid-afternoon and will soon continue till midnight if Belle has her way.

When the mistral blows, I put on my Damart arctic underwear and get so hot I have to go somewhere to take off my tights. I usually choose an underground car park in Toulon, a hazardous place because of the local custom of robbing folk when they step out of their car or descend the staircase towards the ticket machines, purse in hand!

The greatest hazard in French underground car parks, however, is not robbers but getting lost. It can take so long to find the exit that the buzzer sounds when you insert your 'paid' ticket to lift the barrier. When that happens, the guard appears, asks why you haven't paid the fee and looks menacing. It happened to me once near the port in Toulon. When I explained that I had been driving around for half an hour searching for the exit, my accent and appearance of being truly incapable of finding my way to the street disarmed the guard and he let me pay the excess and leave. Since then I've had a lurking fear of car parks that makes staying at home a real pleasure.

This house is old and full of nooks and crannies. There isn't a right angle in the place and the stair treads were made for the feet of tiny early-nineteenth-century residents. The result is that many visitors come a cropper and have to eat a large dinner and stay the night to recover from the shock. The exterior walls are a metre thick, the despair of plumbers and masons. The street is parallel to the main thoroughfare of the village but one level lower.

We're lucky to have all the shops within a hundred yards but unlucky to be the house at the junction of two streets. Tourists often shout their anger at Monsieur for not having warned them that they could hit a wall, get their car stuck in the rain drain or displace one of the metal grids that cover the under-street entries. These make a terrible noise when displaced and can do a lot of harm to cars. Monsieur, who does the stiff upper lip better than any English gentleman, does not reply and if they get too offensive he ups and returns to the house.

In the Midi, tourists who shout at the locals are always surprised when doors close and people become invisible. When someone lovely appears, however, such as a young American who got her front wheel stuck in the rain channel and cried because she couldn't get it out, the street filled, as if by magic, with muscled men who lifted her *and* her car out! The Latin is a gentleman when he chooses to be, but never with rude people.

The Mayor of our village, a handsome chap much admired by everyone, has recently installed screw-in metal bollards to prevent parking in the main square. As the villagers don't much like walking with heavy shopping bags, the measure has provoked a new phenomenon: the daring, high-speed right turn. Many villagers have bought smaller cars. Already lots of ladies, including old ladies, have Vespas or motorbikes. They can all be seen advancing up the main street and then turning at a brutally sharp angle of ninety degrees towards the kerb to park between two bollards. Young and old do it and the bollards are barely resented. The word for 'bollard' in French is *'borne'*, but hereabouts they call them *'bittes'*, which is the French slang for your willy.

The elderly of the region never fail to astound and touch me. They walk upright, carry their shopping bags themselves and don't consider themselves aged until they're over eighty and even then they look only sixty. One old lady from Arles sold her house on a *'viager'* arrangement to a local lawyer. This gave her a small lump sum and a substantial monthly rent that paid for her place in an old people's home. She was well over eighty when she did the deal, so the lawyer thought he'd made a wonderfully astute purchase. The lady died recently at 123. The lawyer had died before her!

At the start of the February holidays, when the French go to the mountains to ski and return with a broken leg, La Cadière d'Azur is beautiful. Almond blossom comes out, white against the stark black boughs, the wisteria starts to bud and lemon trees fruit. This is a village for cat lovers and February and March are the cat courting season with males disputing territory and females getting chased around the pepper tree in the garden next door.

The Brigade love the garden and can be seen from my bedroom window chasing around like dervishes. A morning among the ferns and flowers, climbing trees or leaping from one wall to the next, ensures their healthy appetites and the deafening roar of their snoring all afternoon and every night. Noir sometimes falls asleep right there in the garden, returning home only when he wishes to use his scratch box. I have never before known a cat who likes his scratch box better than a nearby garden. Except Noir, who can often be seen rushing home when his bladder or bowels call.

We had visitors in the spring, a married couple of impeccable elegance and upright nature. They stayed in the local hostellerie, as all bedrooms here are prone to nocturnal feline visits. Then, in late morning, they came for coffee and stayed on for lunch. They were long-time friends of Monsieur and talked animatedly, while I went upstairs to the kitchen to check I hadn't burned the lunch.

Belle was in a villainous mood because when there's no one around she likes to lie at full stretch on the dining table, a forbidden pursuit that she thoroughly enjoys. The arrival of our guests had necessitated pretty table settings, flowers and fuss and there was no place for a Siamese rabbit-cat. Belle got into such a fury, she vomited on my place mat. I am a patient woman, so I didn't strangle her, just changed everything, redid the table and put Belle on to the window ledge to watch the street scene.

Lunch went well. Belle slept like a log till the guests were eating second helpings of black chocolate ganache. Then, waking and hearing voices, she took a turn or two or three around the table, before springing up and miaowing a protest at the noise, the interruption of her precious routines and the occupation of *her* table.

Always the model of diplomacy, Monsieur suggested coffee in the snug and led his guests downstairs. I cleared the table, switched on the washing machine and then took Belle in my arms. Within seconds she was giving me her idea of affection, head knocks to the nose and front teeth that are her way of 'kissing'. She purred contentedly when I cleared the table and was happy to lie down on it and fall asleep. Relieved, I hurried to join the guests.

On entering, I stopped dead before a highly erotic and comic scene. The guests were drinking coffee. Dodu, who had taken a great fancy to the military style of the husband, was lying on her back on the day bed next to his armchair, her four paws in the air, her eyes on his in a display of coquetry that would have earned an X certificate from the censor in my youth. The gentleman tried to continue his polite conversation, but became more and more astonished and hypnotised by Dodu's behaviour. Monsieur looked appealingly at me, as if to say 'Do something.' I did nothing at all except drink my coffee, too riveted to see what Dodu would dream up next. Finally, she undulated gently from side to side, her eyes still on the gentleman visitor. He kept looking anxiously at his wife, who, thank heavens, had a marvellous sense of humour. He looked even more anxiously at Dodu, who by now was giving him her version of the full Monty, complete with geisha eyes. The spell was broken when, lulled by all the erotic undulations, Dodu fell fast asleep on her back, her four little paws still in the air.

When our guests had gone, Monsieur looked sternly at Dodu, whose sensuality, football skills and desire to eat his glasses have always irritated him.

'That cat must be left upstairs when we have guests. They can meet Lunette or Pink Nose.'

'I'll remember, but don't complain when Lunette lets rip one of her supersonic, stereophonic farts while everyone's drinking his coffee or Pink Nose bites some-one's ear because she doesn't like strangers.'

Sighing wearily, Monsieur put on his earphones and listened to Gregorian chants for the rest of the after-noon. He loves music for funerals and what I irreverently call *miserabilis miserabilis*. My love of turbu-lent music by Russian or Central European composers is not shared by my husband. The only music we both like is military marches, and often passers-by in the street can see two ramrod-straight 'soldiers' marching in the snug, followed by six excited cats.

A few days later workmen came to do some repairs on the second floor of the house. No one realised that, once they started breaking down the old wall, there would be a mass evacuation of the scorpion population. The following morning I was bitten on the bottom as I plumped down on my bed to answer the phone. Less then a week later I was bitten again near the knee. Both injuries swelled to spectacular dimensions and turned purple, necessitating visits from the doctor and injections in case of this or that or God knows what.

At first Monsieur refused absolutely to believe that there were scorpions in the house. And when I went to notify the workmen that they must take care not to be injured, because the scorpion and cockroach population was obviously in fine form, they laughed delightedly at my accent and said that stories of scorpions were just village gossip. The foreman, a fine fellow with legs like tree trunks, told me he'd never seen scorpions in all his years in the region.

We had an unaccustomed cold spell during the days that followed and I took to serving Irish coffee after the workmen had finished their packed lunches. This was greatly appreciated and sometimes on a Friday I served seconds. It was in the middle of their Friday Irish coffee session that I heard a piercing howl, followed by shouts and frenzied hammer blows. I ran to the garage in time to witness three men inspecting the foreman's bottom, which was swelling before their eyes like a slowly inflated balloon. The fourth workman was beating the daylights out of a large black scorpion.

I said, not expecting to be believed, as they considered female writers to be creatures of excessive imagination, 'Do take care. Scorpions usually walk around in twos.'

The foreman accepted a third Irish coffee and replied

with as much dignity as he could muster, 'If I see another I'll give him three arseholes with my Black & Decker, madame.'

From that moment on, in my bedroom, I used sprays to render the 'enemies' slow witted. And in coffee and lunch breaks the masons in the garage pursued scorpions. When they caught one and killed it, they placed the body in a big jam jar, which soon resembled a surrealist sculpture. I remembered the story told by Françoise Gilot, of when she and Picasso lived in Menerbes. Once, on returning home after dinner with friends, Picasso had adored seeing her waiting to enter the house, a circle of scorpions like a crown, behind her on the wall.

A few days later it became obvious that Dodu was ill. She lay prostrate, visibly shocked, her head supported by the edge of the day bed. She didn't rush to me when I arrived for my coffee in the early hours of the morning, just lay staring into space as if terrified speechless with pain or both.

I ate breakfast in record time, got out the basket for transporting the cats to the vet's surgery and was there with Dodu at eight thirty, when Dr Feat arrived to start his day. He examined Dodu and agreed that she was in shock, but didn't know why. He administered an anti-toxin and told me to return with her the following day. I drove home with Dodu at my side, wondering how she could have become so ill when she had been perfectly well the evening before. It was a lovely day and I drove on the coast road, but I got no pleasure from the sight of the sea and the sky, beautiful as they were, because Dodu was ill, perhaps very ill. A sick animal is the saddest of situations. As they can't describe what ails them but depend on us to help, the result is sleepless nights and anguish.

On arrival at the house, I backed into the garage and lifted Dodu's basket out of the rear of the car. I was about to put it on the floor when I noticed a scorpion next to my right foot. I knew then what had happened. Dodu and the rest of the Brigade, with the exception of Timi, sleep in baskets placed on chests of drawers or on cushions on the roof of the car. And there were still scorpions about, despite the workmen's efforts, because Monsieur had not wanted the house sprayed, even with products specially formulated to be animal and people friendly. Monsieur doesn't like sprays because they make his nose run and I don't like to upset him. But this was an emergency. I went at once to tell him what I'd seen.

'I've discovered what made Dodu ill.'

'And what was it?'

I handed him the dead scorpion wrapped in a bit of old newspaper. Monsieur sighed when I spoke.

'I'm going to spray the garage and then the whole house. We're lucky it's a lovely day. We'll have a special picnic lunch outside with the cats so your nose doesn't overflow.'

After the spraying process, I did my best to make the two-hour wait to return to the house interesting and had magazines, orange juice, champagne and mushroom quiches to indulge Monsieur. As for the Brigade, we went to the garden and gathered stones, took photos and raced each other from wall to wall, before returning to play water games around the street tap. I got so carried away I filled my shoes with water. The leather dye ran and I had jet-black feet by the end of the morning.

Finally we all went back into the house. I carried Dodu, still prostrate and dull-eyed, and that night she slept on the day bed so Monsieur could keep watch over her. It took three days for her to get over the shock and nearly a week to fully recover, by which time she had started to enjoy the invalid's life, being carried everywhere by her mistress and having special chicken lunches. She's well now but the experience has left its mark and she is more fearful of doing things alone. She still eats Monsieur's glasses, still sleeps with her paws in the air and is the most affectionate member of the Brigade.

Whenever I take an umbrella out of the house, I leave it somewhere. This is because I was born in a town where eighty-mile-per-hour gales were normal and umbrellas were rarely used in case they turned their owners into Mary Poppins and provoked a flight into the sea. Unused as I am to umbrellas, Monsieur insists that I use one if there's a downpour.

One early morning, I left a rose-pink Soleiado umbrella in the bar, after I'd had my lemon tea and brioche. It had stopped raining by the time I left so I didn't notice that I'd forgotten the umbrella. In truth, I was delighted to be rid of it when I did realise, because I usually buy black umbrellas made for tight-arsed city gentlemen. The Soleiado had been a gift from a friend who obviously thought I was the flowery type.

Later in the morning, I returned to the main street to pick up a cooked chicken from the butcher's. It began to rain and suddenly I saw Monsieur Auguste walking up the street holding my rose-pink umbrella to shield his head, tweed cap and baggy trousers from the downpour. He looked so happy with his twirly black moustache and twinkling eyes, both in fascinating contrast to the froufrou umbrella, that I just said, '*Bonjour*, Monsieur Auguste.' He replied, with a roguish smile, '*Bonjour*, Madame Hélène.' Then he moved on, proud as a peacock, towards his home with all the style of Charles Trénet in his straw hat. Our village is full of stylish characters and I adore all of them, but there'll never be another like Auguste.

Just before my departure for London, Monsieur read that there was torrential rain in England. He therefore insisted that I take his umbrella with me on the plane. Nothing would dissuade him from the idea, so I took it.

It was a memorable journey. On rising to leave the plane at Heathrow, I hoisted my bag over my right shoulder and carried the umbrella gripped in the centre like a rifle. I immediately offended the Frenchman standing in front of me, because I'd accidentally slid the point of the umbrella between his legs and had been violating his civil rights for five minutes before he turned to protest. Then the stewardess announced that we must leave by the rear door of the plane. Everyone turned and some began pushing. This time I slid the point of the umbrella between the same man's thighs, but from the front and not the rear. This time he let out a high-pitched shriek that made me momentarily fearful that I'd punctured his importance!

I never travelled with an umbrella again and Monsieur never asked me to. Sometimes, he asks me to tell him the story of my journey to London with his umbrella, so he can laugh like a child whenever it rains.

Chapter Fifteen

The reason why I chose my house was that it stood next to the magic garden. This belonged to an old lady who often sat on the front terrace, talking to passing friends about the garden, the changes in the village or her legendary constipation. The lady owned her own house, situated at one side of the magic garden, and also the house adjoining mine, both at a distance of forty metres across the stone paths, flowers and enchantment she had created.

The magic garden was like something out of a fairytale. The pergola was heavy with old-fashioned pink roses and a fifty-year-old wisteria climbed along the adjacent house wall and then trespassed, to my delight, along mine, continuing as far as my front door. Perfumes of wisteria, rose, jasmine and thyme filled the summer evening air and often I stood at the window of my room looking in awe at the beauty of the ancient pepper tree, the giant datura and endless little dry-stone paths that led to the well, the cellar and, in my fertile imagination, the secret underground passages between the two houses of the Old Lady of the South.

The magic garden was the domain of Patcat, a strange and mysterious animal, whom no one could pick up and who had never been known to purr. Other cats could enter the garden only if Patcat allowed them to and she had been known to defend her territory with tigerlike ferocity. Patcat was black with white feet and the eyes of Shere Khan, Kipling's wily jungle predator. She walked alone, silent, never looking to left or right but seeing everything. For years I had passed the wrought-iron gates of her garden domain and said 'Bonjour, Patcat' if she was sitting on the other side watching the world pass by. Patcat never once gave a sign of having seen me or of feeling the slightest desire to know me.

One day, the old lady died and the two houses and the magic garden were inherited by several of her nieces and nephews. Nothing changed except that the family who had rented the house adjoining mine and who had been responsible for maintaining the garden, left. The elfin-faced wife, Christine, had organised the move with her usual efficiency. On the day of the move, she, her husband and son, Leo, who adored Patcat, left the house with Sekotine, their second cat. Patcat was nowhere to be found. She didn't wish to move. The magic garden was her world and she wanted to stay there. Christine and Leo came back often, sometimes twice a week for more than a year. But Patcat remained hidden in her mysterious wild world. And little by little the magic garden became a jungle. A winter of cloudbursts made everything grow waist high, especially the weeds. I loved it more than ever, inventing stories that took place in this enchanted kingdom of exotic perfumes.

On a grey day in autumn, I could no longer resist the temptation and, climbing over the wall, entered the magic garden. I walked to the well and saw that it had long been filled in. There were rare snail shells on the ground all around and I gathered a few of these to use in one of my collage pictures. Then I went to the terrace and sat looking out and wondering where Patcat was. Her reputation for biting, scratching and being aggressive was frightening, so I'd brought a present, in case of an unexpected encounter.

I was scanning every inch of the far side of the garden, when I realised that Patcat was sitting on the stone step, not far from me, so I pulled the chicken croquettes from my pocket and gave them to her. Patcat ate with relish, but when I tried to stroke her head she scratched my hand so it bled. Discouraged, I went off to search for more shells and found at least thirty. Patcat followed at a distance, her hooded eyes following my every move. In her silent, menacing way, she was magnificent.

A week later, I climbed into the garden, as I had each day, this time followed by the Brigade. I watched as Noir and then each of his sisters went to Patcat, touched noses out of respect and were allowed to proceed wherever they wanted. I decided not to touch noses with Patcat, in case of losing an eye, but gave her some croquettes, as usual. I took two rolls of photographs of the Brigade that day and then threw tiny stones for them to retrieve, a game they all adore. Dodu can dribble like Pele and carry things in her mouth like a champion retriever from Cruft's. She ran back and forth, in hot competition with her brother and with Lunette, who also likes retrieving but who has to be discouraged from swallowing what she's found.

It was some time before I realised that Patcat wanted

me to throw a pebble for her. I did, but I was too afraid of her claws to compete with her to retrieve it. Still, she played with the Brigade and, from a distance, with me until we returned home to sit on the house steps with the dog of my neighbour. Etalon loves sitting on the steps, watching the cats play, having a bone and being a good boy. That afternoon, he kept looking questioningly at me and I wondered why he seemed uncertain. Then Monsieur appeared and said, 'Well, I never saw that before!' and, turning, I saw Patcat sitting on my left, calmly watching the passing scene. I ignored her completely, in case of provoking her 'scratch everyone' reaction and she remained there for over an hour. Then, suddenly, she was gone.

Rumour had it that the two houses and the magic garden were for sale, but no one appeared and everything remained as it always had been. Patcat had a lovely spring and summer in her garden and often the Brigade and I went to sit on the wall in the afternoon sun, so we could try to get to know her. She never came to me, though, preferring to climb the false acacia tree in the heat of the day. Then, hidden from view and shaded from the sun, she slept. It was obvious that Patcat loved two things most in all the world: her tree and the flower-hung terrace of the garden, which formed the very heart of her territory and her life.

I had had time now to observe Patcat in detail and to understand her routines. In the morning, she slept late in the cellar of the house adjacent to mine, emerging around eleven and entering the garden by a hole in the cellar wall. After a saunter around to find something to eat, she climbed on to the roof of the henhouse and lay in the sun for an hour, stretching her limbs and loving every minute of it. When the sun became uncomfortably hot, she either played with the Brigade or climbed her tree until it was time to go to her late-afternoon vantage point on the world, behind the bougainvillea of the terrace. Always she sought to be invisible, to observe without being observed.

One day, when I arrived in the garden, Patcat jumped down from behind the flowers and stood looking expectantly up at me. Was she hungry? What did she want? I hurried away and prepared a plate of food and gave it to her. Patcat ate and then walked back, at a safe distance from me, to the house. She returned, swift as an arrow, to her garden the moment I opened my front door. This ceremony became a habit and for weeks Patcat ate, walked me home and then ran back to her kingdom.

Finally, a neighbour told Monsieur that the two houses and the magic garden had been bought by the Town Council, so the small modern house could be used as temporary classrooms while the village school was being extended. Since the arrival of the new and go-ahead Mayor and the construction of a motorway link between Saint-Cyr and Toulon, including exit and entrance that served La Cadière d'Azur, our village had become a very desirable place to live. It was no longer the poor relation of Le Castellet. Indeed, many residents of that village, exhausted by the volume of tourists, had sold up and come to La Cadière d'Azur. The new Mayor organised teams of gardeners, painters and craftsmen to repair, replant and repaint, and suddenly what had seemed to some, though not to me, to be a sombre village became a beautiful place to live. People appreciated the 'real village life' and lack of tourist hordes. Some rented the same house every year for the summer and many, who had formerly worked in major cities, bought a home in the village, so their children could live in an unpolluted atmosphere. The result of the new image was more young settlers, more children and a whole new infrastructure to create for the education of future Cadièriens. The little house on the other side of the magic garden would be part of the master plan.

Spring came. The Brigade chased after one another and Frioul, the tom cat from the house opposite, got exhausted doing the honours with every female in the area. He grew so thin Monsieur began feeding him in between the copious meals served by his mistress Sylvie, in case he faded clean away.

Patcat observed her routines and was content, until one fine morning, when the roaring of lorries was heard and men opened the wrought-iron gates of the magic garden and rolled in bulldozers and other giant equipment. When I asked what was happening, someone replied, 'A clean-up.'

The lemon tree was the first thing to be destroyed. Then they hacked the wisteria from the walls and carted away the severed fifty-year-old branches in a lorry. Patcat and I watched in horror. Then I ran back home to have a good cry. It wasn't my wisteria, of course, but having been allowed for more than ten years to share it had been the realisation of a dream. I had always wanted a wisteria to scent my bedroom. Wiping my red eyes and red nose, I heard a new noise. Somewhere, men with sledgehammers were demolishing something. I looked out of my bedroom window and saw that the roof of Patcat's henhouse had already fallen, as had part of the walls.

I ran outside and, without thinking of the danger, grabbed Patcat, who was staring in seeming incomprehension at the scene. On one side the henhouse and everywhere else paths were being uprooted, their dry stones carried off on lorries. I carried Patcat to the other side of my house, where we sat together near the neighbour's honeysuckle climber. I didn't say a word, touched when she glanced up at me from time to time and then climbed to my side and sat with her body hidden under my old woolly jacket.

Patcat and I stayed there for a long time, till the workmen left at five thirty. Then we walked slowly to the magic garden and looked at the pile of rubble that had once been Patcat's afternoon resting place. The stone paths were gone and many other trees too, including the mandarin and a lemon tree. The tall pillars of the terrace had been demolished and so had the low wall where I had often sat with her, though the bougainvillea remained. I walked over to it and sat on the ground, wondering how Patcat would surmount the shock and destruction all around.

In the weeks that followed the torture continued. All the plants and flowers disappeared, except the pepper tree, one evergreen and the bougainvillea. Patcat and I watched as the datura and the strawberry bush and the daisy bushes disappeared. The magic circle of evergreens around the well were uprooted and then a tractor was brought in to turn over the earth. In an inexorable trail of destruction, the magic garden died before our eyes. For me it became a memory, to be savoured and longed for, like the scenes in the sepia photos in a much-loved family album. For Patcat, who knows . . .?

She survived, but she walked slowly, her head drooping, her tail between her legs. I was relieved and hopeful that the 'cleaning process' was over, when, one golden morning, Monsieur told me that a tree cutter's lorry was outside the garden. It didn't take long to do what had been ordered and, by the time the expert tree chopper left, what remained of Patcat's afternoon hiding place was two metres of trunk, a souvenir without shade or reason for being. I walked slowly, reluctantly, towards the gate and looked through the iron railings to where Patcat was standing, gazing up at her tree. Her body was rigid and she didn't move despite the cacophony of the work going on all around her.

We all have our ideas of what constitutes an emergency and this was mine. I walked back to the house and explained to Monsieur what we should do. Always calm in disastrous moments, he immediately went to prepare a litter box and find a carton or a basket to be used. I went upstairs and found bowls, food, bedding, enough for two hundred! Then, wondering if I could persuade Patcat to take refuge in the house for a few days, I opened the door to return to search for her. At the same moment, a black and white streak of lightning passed me and went upstairs towards the first-floor landing. Taken by surprise, I closed the door and ran upstairs to check it really was Patcat and, if so, where she was. I couldn't find her. I poured water into the drinking trough and made a great fuss of shaking and arranging the covers in the basket Monsieur had prepared for her. I felt sure she must be watching from somewhere, but where?

Finally, still unable to find Patcat, I went upstairs to the highest point of the house, the guest bedroom, and found her hiding behind an armchair. I didn't try to touch her. I just moved the water and croquettes, the basket and water trough into the guest suite. Then, exhausted by recent events, I flopped down on the edge of the bed, wondering what to do. I thought of all the lovely times I'd had with the Brigade and Patcat in the garden and knew it was over, for always, and must not become a source of perpetual sadness. I'd lost precious people and places before and knew how to handle the anguish of it all, but Patcat was an animal, who had just lost the only world she had ever known. What was worse was that she had watched its destruction daily for weeks. She had never let anyone hold her, kiss her, comfort her. How then could I hope to change her whole way of living? I wanted so much to try, but every time I'd attempted to touch her she'd hurt me. I went over all this for quite a while, startled, when, without warning, Patcat sprang on to my knees and sat gazing into my eyes.

I remained still, wondering if I dared stroke her, and then, putting my arms around her, did just that. And she purred loud and long and purred again and again. It was some time before I put her into her basket, having first shown her around and indicated the litter box, water and food. As she'd only ever slept in the garden, I showed her how to scratch in the box. Then, seeing fatigue in her eyes, I left her alone for a while, disappearing to tell Monsieur all the news, but leaving the door open in case Patcat panicked.

She slept for four days and nights, rising only to use the box, drink water and sit on my knee to be stroked. And each time she purred, as if this strange and unique contact, a pleasure she had never contemplated before, pleased her immensely. She didn't make any attempt to go out and didn't eat, which worried me to death. Her movements were slow, not at all like her usual resolute way. I put the trancelike state down to shock at losing her garden and did my best to offer affection, because it was all I had to give.

I was relieved that Patcat slept for four days, because during that time workmen filled in the hole in the wall that had been her entry to the cellars of the house next door. The cellars were vast and had been Patcat's shelter from winter cold. The pepper tree, the bougainvillea and the evergreen bush remained, but now white wire fences had been erected around the periphery of the land and also around the adjacent house terrace. A line of concrete formed a path through which the children would pass en route to their 'temporary class'. From my upper window, it looked exactly like a prison yard. It was clean, orderly, antiseptic and in accordance with every regulation of the Ministry of Education. The poetry, mystery and beauty were lost for ever and many mourned them, but none more than Patcat and me.

When, finally, Patcat decided to venture out of the house – a Sunday morning, when no children or workmen were there – I walked with her to the garden and we sat on the turned earth together. She showed me that she could slide under the white wire fencing and stand in the sun, hidden behind the bougainvillea, as she always had. I found a few stones and we played together, but not for long. After ten minutes, Patcat returned to her bedroom and settled on the eiderdown Monsieur had bought for her. Patcat loves her eiderdown and is possessive of it. And in the cool of evening, when she's had her walk and her visit to her 'garden', she hurries back for the twilight stroking session that makes her purr. She's seven or eight years old and she never purred before. We both feel she's making up for lost time.

Monsieur said one day he thought it very odd that a fifty-year-old wisteria of great beauty had had to be destroyed to make way for nothing at all but a series of white iron railings. I smile when he says that, because we both know that people who destroy gardens do so in order to cover what was once beautiful with concrete. No one has mentioned this yet.

Chapter Sixteen

The first six months of Patcat's residence in our home were sweet and sour. The good part was watching her sleep on the eiderdown Monsieur had given her and seeing the look of pleasure when she hurried downstairs to eat her favourite breakfast. The difficult part was the mercurial changes of mood that soon became evident. One minute she was happy. Then, if I lifted my hand or made a movement she didn't understand, she returned to being a wildcat and scratched me, as she always had.

Monsieur became adept at disinfecting my wounds. He encouraged me and gave me lots of affection, but Patcat remained on guard, suspicious and defiant. I had made the decision from the beginning not to punish her, not to show anger or shout, simply to give her time to grow accustomed to having a home again and people who loved her. As time passed, even my legendary patience began to falter, so I rethought my behaviour and tried to work out how best to reassure her. I decided that I was wrong in thinking like a woman and not a wildcat. Worse, I wanted civilised behaviour from Patcat, for my convenience. I tried to envisage her life in the three and a half years that she had been alone in the magic garden, returning to the wild and being forever on the defensive. We knew that Patcat wanted to stay, because when she went out she always hurried back and ran upstairs to her quarters. What she didn't yet understand was that I could be trusted never to hurt her.

The next day I bought a tiny ball in the supermarket and took it home, hoping to get Patcat to play. She watched as it bounced by and then turned her back on me. At that moment I noticed a long piece of double Velcro on the floor of her room. I'd been searching for it for ages and picked it up eagerly. Like all Velcro it crackled. Patcat's ears shot up and without warning she took a flying leap to try to take possession of this strange, crinkly-crunkly 'snake'. The game lasted an hour, at the end of which Patcat snuggled up to me on the bed. I stroked her back and tickled her ears and then picked up my writing pad and corrected a few pages. Patcat slept like a child, waking sometime later and hurrying immediately to search for her Velcro under the bed.

I realised at once that our games had given me an identity to Patcat's feline way of thinking. I was no longer a possible danger, an unknown. I was the person who played with her. She began to leap up on to the divan in the studio and lie at my side when I was searching for pieces for my collages or writing a few pages. And each morning she jumped to the roof so she could watch me hosing down the terrace. Not being given to the same passion for water as the Brigade,

Patcat kept well out of the way during the cleaning process. After the terrace, she formed the habit of accompanying me to the bathroom, so she could watch me shower. She did this by perching on top of a cupboard, well away from the jets of water, and she enjoyed every minute of the performance.

When Monsieur came in and saw Patcat spectating, he was astonished.

'Why does she watch you in the shower?'

'She probably finds it amusing. It's part of her morning routine.'

'Next she will come into the lavatory with you!'

'She already does.'

'*Mon Dieu*! I never heard of such a thing. She should be called Glue.'

Monsieur glanced up at Patcat, who remained as impassive as the Sphinx. I kept quiet, avoiding telling my husband that Noir and Dodu also came in the downstairs bathroom to drink running water from the bidet and that both liked coming into the toilet too.

Patcat finally settled completely in the house and proved to be a homebody. Her only fault was her desire to tear up collage papers, which I had to discourage by putting everything into cardboard boxes and covering them with a Flokati. Patcat thought this was a new bed and leapt up on it and slept all day, stopping all collage activity. When she was awake, she 'assisted' with household tasks and that was how I ended up with buttercup-yellow feet.

That day, I put newspapers on the floor and covers on the furniture. Patcat was banished to the mantelpiece before I started to spray the rocking chair yellow. It took quite a time and towards the end I realised that Patcat was sitting too close for comfort. Knowing my lack of expertise and tendency to paint my nose, hair and glasses – and not wanting a yellow cat – I encouraged her to sit on the sofa. Then I hurried to finish spraying.

When Monsieur entered the room, he looked hard at the chair and then said, 'I think it would be nicer in black, but use paint and a brush when you redo it.' Puzzled, I turned to question him and he continued his reasoning: 'You have a very delicate skin that won't like being soaked in white spirit, so it could take some time for your feet to return to their normal colour.'

Looking down, I saw that my feet were vivid buttercup yellow and patterned with a wicker effect, where the paint had penetrated through the rocking-chair seat. At first I laughed at my oversight. Then I thought how lucky I was. In winter I wear tights, so no one would see my yellow feet and ankles. Patcat sniffed my paint-stained feet, then sniffed the rocking chair and bit it hard to vent her annoyance with its alien odour. Then she went upstairs to search for her Velcro, so she could have a quick game before going to bed.

Autumn passed and wintery skies – sometimes grey, sometimes blue, always bright – became the norm. Black branches framed the wondrous view of the vineyards from the top of the hill of La Cadière d'Azur. In summer we complain of the heat, at least by the end of August when sun fatigue sets in. By November we start complaining of the cold, the flu and our Olympic-sized chilblains. I used to have chilblains, but the French have herbal remedies for absolutely everything and since I learned to trust their experts to dose me with phytotheraphy I've never had a red finger or toe.

The Brigade no longer go out in the predawn hours. In winter they venture out around eleven and if Noir decides it's too cold for small animals they all rush back in and lie on Monsieur's bed. Lunette lies on top of the telly, because it's warm, and Dodu gets under the table lamp, despite Monsieur's objection to her long hairs on his polished wood.

At first Patcat wanted to reign alone in the upper part of the house, but, as my room is on the first floor and Timi lives there for most of the day, this resistance to sharing had to be overcome. I didn't know how to tackle the problem with Patcat, who could win the Nobel Prize for obstinacy. I was surprised when Timi found the solution. She is a very timid cat, afraid of everything but with a determination that is unequalled in any other member of the Brigade.

On meeting Patcat for the first time, Timi rubbed noses respectfully and then proceeded to my room. Patcat looked askance but let her pass. The next day Timi rubbed noses again, but instead of letting her pass Patcat blocked her way. I held my breath, wondering if Timi would retreat and return to Monsieur's quarters. I had underestimated her adoration of my bedroom and her willpower under fire. It's hard to say who was more flabbergasted, Patcat or I, when Timi took a flying vertical-take-off leap over the head of her opponent and then proceeded calmly to her room.

The same thing with variations happened five nights running and Patcat lost each time, owing to Timi's unpredictability. Sometimes, she leapt direct over the head of Patcat. Sometimes she took a curving leap that seemed directionalised to the right, but ended up passing Patcat's left ear. It was better than a John McEnroe service: speed, mystification and class. Finally, Patcat stopped blocking Timi's way and remained at a distance observing her rival, occasionally chasing her to establish mastery, but even then she was stymied by Timi's ability to stand still and disappear into thin air.

No one can become 'invisible cat' as fast as Timi and often Patcat and I spent ages searching for her, but we never found her until Timi wanted to be found. These happenings lasted for a couple of months, after which Patcat decided to accept Timi and for her part Timi continued to rub noses with respect. Finally, they became friends. Timi remains watchful of Patcat and Patcat remains awed by Timi's take-offs, but there are no fights, no rancour.

The other members of the Brigade were not so lucky. Only Dodu manages to sit at the top of the stairs snoring gently, without the slightest objection from Patcat. Noir tried to assert his authority and Patcat sent him packing. Lunette made the error of hissing at the older cat and received a clout that stopped her in her tracks. Pink Nose took one look at Patcat and returned to Monsieur's snug, where she is spoiled to death as usual. Belle escaped the kitchen and attacked Patcat. The battle was interrupted by me, with total disregard for life and limb as I separated the combatants. Belle returned to the kitchen. I was covered in antiseptic by Monsieur and then bandaged like the Invisible Man. The following day I created a series of 'hides' for Patcat in case of a repetition of Belle's visit. Patcat loves her 'hides' and has learned the word, so when visitors come I call 'hide' and within seconds even I can't find her.

I discovered one day that Patcat had a lover, a ferocious grey and white male, who strode like Batman down the street, forcing all other males to take flight and fright. From time to time he disappeared with Patcat, who obviously adored him. I never saw her with another male. Then, one day, the grey's owner moved house and went to live far away in Lyons. He'll never return. Patcat goes to their meeting place and waits for hours for Grey to come. Then she goes to his home and stands looking up at the window, where he used to lie like Adonis in the sun. It's taken a very long time for her to recover from the loss of her friend and even now, when she wants him, she goes slowly, sadly, to their place, even though she has realised that he'll not return. On these days I try to compensate for her loss, though I know that I never can.

Patcat has tuna for tea and double Velcro at playtime. Then we lie on the eiderdown in her room and I tell her she's the very best cat in the world. And Patcat purrs. She has a home, love, food and fun. Like Monsieur and me, she's lived long enough to know that you can't have everything.

Chapter Seventeen

Winter's here again and no one wants to go outside to be frozen solid by the icy blasts of the mistral. Dodu goes out and then scratches the window to come back in. Noir does his round and then takes up his post guarding the radiator. Pink Nose and Lunette go to the garage for running races that end in snoring sessions on the cushions in the car. Timi sleeps on the worktable, Patcat on her eiderdown in the guest room and Monsieur and Belle on the day bed in the kitchen – 'Just for five minutes, Hélène, just five minutes.' On particularly cold days the five minutes last half the afternoon.

Nights can be eventful in this area of France. During a certain period a man climbed on the next-door roof to shine a torch in my eyes while I slept. When I told Monsieur about this he said I was dreaming. When winter came that year, the roof man no longer shone his torch, because my doors and windows were closed, but images appeared on the interior walls of my room.

No one believed me and some thought I was making it all up to make them laugh.

It was then that Timi saved my bacon. The first time the images appeared she howled like Noir doing his Geronimo imitation. Then she leapt from one armchair to another and on to the chimney, trying to find out who was in the room with us. Monsieur came upstairs to find out what the noise was and finally believed me about the images, because of Timi. We never found out who it was, just a man with electronic knowledge, I suppose, who wanted to play role games – or perhaps he was a scientist specialising in holograms.

The episode with Timi made me very watchful of a cat's reactions, so one night, when Timi heard a noise outside the house, I dressed and went down to investigate. I arrived in time to find the yucca tree that Monsieur had planted on the left of the front door of the house gone, stolen. The next night on the other side of the house, Pushy and Spot woke Monsieur to inform him that there were goings on outside that he should know about. In the morning, the yucca of our neighbour had gone. Obviously a thief with a yucca fixation!

Then, one dark night, I was snoring peacefully when I heard a loud noise. I was immediately afraid that someone was trying to demolish the garage doors. When three further loud bangs broke the silence of the night, I dressed and ran downstairs to look out of the 'Judas window' in the front door. I was horrified to see flames leaping up from the courtyard of the house facing mine. The owner had emptied her cellar of unwanted everything and left it in a high pile in her open-to-the-street courtyard. A pyromaniac had set light to it, so he/she could see the fire brigade at work. Explosions of aerosol canisters sounded like machine guns. Wood fell from above the fire and fire hoses sprayed blue foam on everything in sight. Neighbours gathered, as if watching a film, and everyone admired the skill and courage of the firemen, whom we had never seen in action before. I was watching from my window when I realised that the fire was immediately opposite the garage where the Brigade sleep. Taking Timi with me, I ran downstairs to liberate them and put them in Monsieur's apartment.

I met Monsieur at the connecting door. He was fully dressed, elegant and cool.

'I've evacuated the garage, Hélène. The Brigade are in my living room with Pushy and Spot. They think it's a very special occasion and are delighted by the treat. I've made coffee, so do come and we'll have an extra-early breakfast.'

Hurrying in with Timi, I was spoiled with a gallon of coffee and some croissants. I ate and drank lying back on the day bed, trying not to spill a drop, despite the fact that the Brigade were taking up position for sleeping, as in the days of their kittenhood. Noir was on my stomach, Dodu near my ear, Timi near the beat of the heart. We all woke at four thirty, by which time the only signs of the fire were blackened doors and beams on the ground floor of the house opposite and dried blue foam that the fireman had used to contain the blaze.

Later, the Brigade took a turn around the courtyard of the house facing mine, but returned almost immediately. Dodu had discovered that charcoal turns white fur black and spent the rest of the day washing herself. Noir had had a taste of the old days, sleeping on my stomach, and he positioned himself as he had in the night and snored peacefully. Pink Nose was a bit unnerved by the departure from her precious routines and had to go and hide under Monsieur's jacket. Lunette ate and ate and ate and Pushy sneezed four hundred times, because the smoke had upset her sinuses.

On Christmas Eve it snowed. Looking out of the window, Monsieur and I saw a thick white carpet over the stark, black, fire-burned outlines of the courtyard opposite. When we watched the television news, we were warned that dozens of cars had been abandoned on the Aix–Toulon motorway. It's always the same story: snow is such a rare occurrence here that life stops, and deliveries of food, journeys, airports and railways all become disorganised until the great meltdown arrives. The fire brigade and emergency services are kept busy hauling cars and their owners out of ditches, fields and vineyards, where speeding drivers had suddenly found themselves 'car-skiing'. There are no snowploughs, or if there are no one knows how to use them. Nothing to do but wait. The locals become philosophical, the men going to the bar for a pastis, the women cooking up a storm to put everyone in a good humour.

At midday, two American friends appeared, exhausted, having walked for miles from their abandoned cars. We put them in the spare bedroom and Monsieur served champagne to cheer them up. I started cooking, in case of an invasion by fifty people all lost in the snowstorm. In fact only two more arrived, an English couple who'd travelled the world and had therefore quickly abandoned all idea of continuing on to Nice, arriving instead, minus their car and mauve with cold. Monsieur served more champagne and I set the dinner table and served giant dishes of pasta with seafood sauce, seven cheeses and a sticky dessert guaranteed to put kilos on anyone, even anorexics! Our guests began to relax and lose their mauve complexions.

They all retired early, the English couple sleeping on the spare bed in the kitchen, because we have only one guest room. Monsieur bade them goodnight, remarking to me afterwards that we were lucky Belle was asleep or she might have eaten them both for trespassing on *her* territory.

When the house was silent, I went and checked that the cats were sleeping peacefully, despite the arrival of the snow, which had surprised them, to say the least. I found everyone except Noir, who wasn't in his basket. First Monsieur and I searched the house. Then I, who hate the cold, went out in the snow to look for him, singing his own 'call sign', to which he always responds. I heard Monsieur in the next street doing the same, but Noir was nowhere to be found. Had he slipped away when the two couples arrived and found himself locked out of the house in glacial conditions? If not, where was he?

Having searched the house, I went to bed but couldn't sleep. In the early hours of the morning I got up and went searching again. I met Monsieur doing the same, he in his apartment, I in the street outside the house. At 4 a.m. we sat drinking coffee together and wondering where home-loving Noir had gone. I was afraid he was dead and couldn't hold back the tears.

We let the Brigade in and they all fell asleep again on Monsieur's bed. In the garage, they have their personal baskets, but Monsieur's bed is one of their favourite spots, mainly because it's absolutely forbidden to go there. I went to the garage and changed their water, refilled their dish of croquettes and then turned to Monsieur and asked, 'What's that funny noise?'

'I was wondering too,' he replied. He looked under the washing machine and then under the car, but couldn't source the strange rumbling noise. It was then that I saw Noir lying on the cushions in the back of the car, snoring like a hundred-year-old dinosaur. We picked him up and kissed him. He didn't wake. Monsieur said, 'He seems stupefied!' I began to worry that he was ill, until we found the remains of the last bottle of champagne spilled on the floor of the passage to the garage. No one had noticed it, except Noir, who likes chocolate tart, orange wine and champagne if he can find it.

On New Year's Day we watched the concert from Vienna. I've watched it every year for decades and I still leap up and dance when they play the 'Blue Danube' waltz. On this particular day the room didn't seem big enough, so I waltzed right out into the street where I was relieved that the only watchers were two dogs and the tom cat who lives opposite. Afterwards, Monsieur opened the champagne and toasted the New Year and our families. All went well till the finale of the programme and the traditional rendering of 'The Radetzky March' when all the stately Viennese clap hands on being signalled to do so by the conductor. Monsieur and I don't clap hands: we march; and on this occasion we were in full military formation, ramrod straight and laughing like gongs, when we realised that a group of tourists were watching us from the window, staring open-mouthed at the spectacle within. I called out 'Happy New Year' and they replied with the same. Then, as the programme credits rolled, Monsieur and I lay on the day bed, recuperating from the exertion and Noir, Dodu, Pink Nose and Quixote joined us, unable to resist a spell on the bed with the master and mistress. When everyone was comfortable, Timi arrived and, ever the exception, insisted on sitting to the right of my ear, so she could purr and 'talk' at close quarters. Monsieur closed his eyes, deeply content. We were both happy in a simple, homely way and we loved it.

The following day we ate breakfast with our guests in the kitchen, which is also our dining room. Afterwards, we all went to look at the magic garden, which was no longer the magic garden. The Brigade wanted to play chasing stones, but discovered that walking in snow makes your feet freeze, so they hared off back to the house with the guests, leaving Monsieur and me alone. Looking up at my husband, I saw him watching something in the garden.

'Look, Hélène, Patcat is in her tree. It's growing again, slowly, so she's climbed up to her new hiding place.'

We went into the garden and looked at Patcat in her tree, her face lit by the wintry sun. Snow or not, iron bars or not, she still loved her magic place. Soon, the Brigade will begin the third year of their life and Patcat her second year as our special guest. As we walked back to the house, I saw her hurrying behind and, when we entered, she ran upstairs to her room. It was time for breakfast and she likes her routines and her moments in *her* haven. On this seasonal morning she wanted affection, so we sat on the bed and I stroked her and told her all the things we'd do in the New Year.

To you, yours, and all the cats reading this book, an affectionate *au revoir* from this ancient village in Provence.